Wor/d of Dance

Ballet

Robin Rinaldi

CHELSEA HOUSE
P U B L I S H E R S
A Haights Cross Communications Company

Frontispiece: Vaslav Nijinsky's 1913 ballet *Le Sacre du Printemps* (*Rite of Spring*), with an accompanying score by Igor Stravinsky, was a piece that audiences at the time simply were not ready to accept, closing within a year of its debut. It would not be performed again until 1988.

CHELSEA HOUSE PUBLISHERS
VP, NEW PRODUCT DEVELOPMENT Sally Cheney
DIRECTOR OF PRODUCTION Kim Shinners
CREATIVE MANAGER Takeshi Takahashi
MANUFACTURING MANAGER Diann Grasse

Staff for BALLET
EDITOR Ben Kim
PRODUCTION ASSISTANT Megan Emery
PICTURE RESEARCHER Pat Holl
SERIES & COVER DESIGNER Terry Mallon
LAYOUT 21st Century Publishing and Communications, Inc.

A Haights Cross Communications ⚹ Company

www.chelseahouse.com

First Printing

1 3 5 7 9 8 6 4 2

Library of Congress Cataloging-in-Publication Data

Rinaldi, Robin.
  Ballet/Robin Rinaldi.
    p. cm.—(World of dance)
  Includes index.
  Summary: An introduction to ballet, discussing the history, styles, and famous dancers and choreographers.
    ISBN 0-7910-7640-7 (Hardcover)   0-7910-7773-X (PB)
  1. Ballet—Juvenile literature. [1. Ballet.] I. Title. II. Series.
  GV1787.5.R55 2003
  792.8—dc21
                                                          2003009328

World of Dance

African Dance
Asian Dance
Ballet
European Dance
Middle Eastern Dance
Modern Dance

Table of Contents

Introduction

Elizabeth A. Hanley

Associate Professor of Kinesiology, Penn State University

Dance has existed from time immemorial. It has been an integral part of celebrations and rituals, a means of communication with gods and among humans, and a basic source of enjoyment and beauty.

Dance is a fundamental element of human behavior and has evolved over the years from primitive movement of the earliest civilizations to traditional ethnic or folk styles, to the classical ballet and modern dance genres popular today. The term 'dance' is a broad one and, therefore, is not limited to the genres noted above. In the 21st century, dance includes ballroom, jazz, tap, aerobics, and a myriad of other movement activities.

The richness of cultural traditions observed in the ethnic, or folk, dance genre offers the participant, as well as the spectator, insight into the customs, geography, dress, and religious nature of a particular people. Originally passed on from one generation to the next, many ethnic, or folk, dances continue to evolve as our civilization and society changes. From these quaint beginnings of traditional dance, a new genre emerged as a way to appeal to the upper level of society: ballet. This new form of dance rose quickly in popularity and remains so today. The genre of ethnic, or folk, dance continues to be an important part of ethnic communities throughout the United States, particularly in large cities.

When the era of modern dance emerged as a contrast and a challenge to the rigorously structured world of ballet, it was not readily accepted as an art form. Modern dance was interested in the communication of emotional experiences—through basic movement, through uninhibited movement—not through the academic tradition of ballet masters. Modern dance, however, found its aficionados and is a popular art form today.

No dance form is permanent, definitive, or ultimate. Change occurs but the basic element of dance endures. Dance is for all people. One need only recall that dance needs neither common race nor common language for communication; it has been a universal means of communication forever.

The WORLD OF DANCE series provides a starting point for readers interested in learning about ethnic, or folk, dances of world cultures, as well as the art forms of ballet and modern dance. This series will feature an overview of the development of these dance genres, from an historical perspective to a practical one. Highlighting specific cultures, their dance steps and movements, their customs and traditions, will underscore the importance of these fundamental elements for the reader. Ballet and modern dance, more recent artistic dance genres, are explored in detail as well, giving the reader a comprehensive knowledge of their past, present, and potential future.

The one fact that each reader should remember is that dance has always been, and always will be, a form of communication. This is its legacy to the world.

In this volume, Janet S. Anderson will examine the the fascinating journey and development of modern dance—a relatively young art form that began at the turn of the twentieth century. Pioneers such as Loie Fuller, Isadora Duncan and Ruth St. Denis would break from such dance traditions as ballet, but would also have to fight to gain critical acceptance of their artistic expression. Others would expand upon the abstraction and attention to isolated movement, but modern dance would eventually not only reconcile with ballet, but would also incorporate many other dance styles into its palette.

Foreword

Jacques D'Amboise
Founder, National Dance Institute

"In song and dance, man expresses himself as a member of a higher community. He has forgotten how to walk and speak and is on the way into flying into the air, dancing. . . . his very gestures express enchantment."

—Friedrich Nietzsche

On Maria Dancing by Robert Burns

How graceful Maria leads the dance!
She's life itself. I never saw a foot
So nimble and so elegant; it speaks,
And the sweet whispering poetry it makes
Shames the musicians.

In a conversation with Balanchine discussing the definition of dance, we evolved the following description: "Dance is an expression of time and space, using the control of movement and gesture to communicate."

Dance is central to the human being's expression of emotion. Every time we shake someone's hand, lift a glass in a toast, wave goodbye, or applaud a performer . . . we are doing a form of dance. We live in a universe of time and space, and dance is an art form invented by human beings to express and convey emotions. Dance is profound.

There are melodies that, when played, will cause your heart to droop with sadness for no known reason. Or a rousing jig or mazurka will have your foot tapping in an accompanying rhythm, seemingly beyond your control. The emotions, contacted through music, spur the body to react physically. Our bodies have just been programmed to express emotions. We dance for many reasons: for religious rituals from the most ancient times; for dealing with sadness, tearfully swaying and holding hands at wake; for celebrating weddings, joyfully spinning in circles; for entertainment; for dating and mating. How many millions of couples through the ages have said, "We met at a dance"? But most of all, we dance for joy, often exclaiming, "How I love to dance!" Oh, the JOY OF DANCE!!

I was teaching dance at a boarding school for emotionally disturbed children, ages 9 through 16. They were participating with 20 other schools in the National Dance Institute's (NDI) year-round program. The boarding school children had been traumatized in frightening and mind-boggling ways. There were a dozen students in my class, and the average attention span may have been 15 seconds—which made for a raucous bunch. This was a tough class.

One young boy, an 11-year-old, was an exception. He never took his eyes off of me for the 35 minutes of the dance class, and they were blazing blue eyes—electric, set in a chalk white face. His body was slim, trim, superbly proportioned . . . and he stood arrow-straight. His lips were clamped in a rigid, determined line as he learned and executed every dance step with amazing skill. His concentration was intense despite the wild cavorting, noise, and otherwise disruptive behavior supplied by his fellow classmates.

At the end of class I went up to him and said, "Wow, can you dance. You're great! What's your name?"

Those blue eyes didn't blink. Then he parted his ridged lips and bared his teeth in a grimace that may have been a smile. He had a big hole where his front teeth should be. I covered my shock and didn't let it show. Both top and bottom incisors had been worn away by his continual grinding and rubbing of them together. One of the supervisors of the school rushed over to me and said, "Oh, his name is Michael. He's very intelligent but he doesn't speak."

I heard Michael's story from the supervisor. Apparently, when he was a toddler in his playpen, he witnessed his father shooting his mother—then putting the gun to his own head, the father killed himself. It was close to three days before the neighbors broke in to find the dead and swollen bodies of his parents. The dehydrated and starving little boy was stuck in his playpen, sitting in his own filth. The orphaned Michael disappeared into the foster care system, eventually ending up in the boarding school. No one had ever heard him speak.

In the ensuing weeks of dance class, I built and developed choreography for Michael and his classmates. In the spring, they were scheduled to dance in a spectacular NDI show called *The Event of the Year*. At the boarding school, I used Michael as the leader and as a model for the others and began welding all of the kids together, inventing a vigorous and energetic dance to utilize their explosive energy. It took a while, but they were coming together, little by little over the months. And through all that time, the best in the class—the determined and concentrating Michael—never spoke.

That spring, dancers from the 22 different schools with which the NDI had dance programs were scheduled to come together at Madison Square Garden for *The Event of the Year*. There would be over 2,000 dancers, a symphony orchestra, a jazz orchestra, a chorus, Broadway stars, narrators, and Native American Indian drummers. There was scenery that was the length of an entire city block, and visiting guest children from six foreign countries coming to dance with our New York City children. All of these elements had to come together and fit into a spectacular performance, with only one day of rehearsal. The foremost challenge was how to get 2,000 dancing children on stage for the opening number.

At NDI, we have developed a system called "The Runs." First, we divide the stage into a grid with colored lines making the outlines of box shapes, making a mosaic of patterns and shapes on the stage floor. Each outlined box holds a class from one of the schools, which would consist of 15 to 30 children. Then, we add various colored lines as tracks, starting offstage and leading to the boxes. The dancers line up in the wings, hallways, and various holding areas on either side of the stage. At the end of the overture, they burst onto stage, running and leaping and following their colored tracks to their respective boxes, where they explode into the opening dance number.

We had less than three minutes to accomplish "The Runs." It's as if a couple of dozen trains coming from different places and traveling on different tracks all arrived at a station at the same time, safely pulling into their allotted spaces. But even before starting, it would take us almost an hour just to get the dancers lined up in the correct holding areas offstage, ready to make their entrance. We had scheduled one shot to rehearse the opening. It had to work the first time or we would have to repeat everything. That meant going into overtime at a great expense.

I gave the cue to start the number. The orchestra, singers, lights, and stagehands all commenced on cue, and the avalanche of 2,000 children were let loose on their tracks. "The Runs" had begun!

After about a minute, I realized something was wrong. There was a big pileup on stage left and children were colliding into each other and bunching up behind some obstacle. I ran over to discover the source of the problem—Michael and his classmates. He had ignored everything and led the group from his school right up front, as close to the audience as he could get. Inspiring his dancing buddies, they were a crew of leaping, contorting demons—dancing up a storm, but blocking some 600 other dancers trying to get through.

I rushed up to them yelling, "You're in the wrong place! Back up! Back up!"

Michael—with his eyes blazing, mouth open, and legs and arms spinning in dance movements like an eggbeater—yelled out, "Oh, I am so happy! I am so happy! Thank you Jacques! Oh, it's so good! I am so happy!"

I backed off, stunned into silence. I sat down in the first row of the audience to be joined by several of the supervisors, teachers, and chaperones from Michael's school, our mouths open in wonder. The spirit of dance had taken over Michael and his classmates. No one danced better or with more passion in the whole show that night and with Michael leading the way—the JOY OF DANCE at work. (We went into overtime but so what!)

1

The Human Body as Art

"Dance is the only art in which we ourselves are the stuff of which it is made."

—dancer and choreographer Ted Shawn

WHAT IS BALLET?

Many of us have seen ballet being performed in some form. Perhaps it was a Christmas performance of *The Nutcracker*, either seen live or on television. Perhaps you or someone you know took ballet classes as a child, or is even a professional dancer. But what is so unique about this form of dance that seems so graceful and orderly?

All ballet is dance, but not all dance is ballet. Ballet is a very specific and prescribed sort of dancing. Dance has existed almost as long as humans have walked the earth, but ballet is only 400 years old. Anyone can put on some music, move his or her body to its rhythm, and call it dancing. However, it takes years

The Nutcracker is one of the best-known ballets, traditionally performed during the Christmas season by professional and amateur dancers alike, as well as broadcast on television. Here it is performed by Mikhail Baryshnikov and Gelsey Kirkland.

to train a body into the relatively few positions that make up ballet's vocabulary of steps. Dance can happen in the street, in a house, in a school gymnasium, or basically anywhere. A ballet, however, only takes place in a theater or at least on some sort of stage. Many people teach themselves to dance, but virtually nobody can learn ballet the way some teach themselves to act, paint, sing, or play guitar. It must be learned in a school under the tutelage of a highly trained teacher.

Ballet is the most academic form of theatrical dance, and the most difficult to learn and perform. Most professional dancers—not only ballerinas but Broadway performers and modern dancers as well—have been trained in ballet as a foundation. Gymnasts and figure skaters often study ballet as well. National Football League coaches have even been known to send their players to ballet class for strength training.

Ballet dancers are fond of quoting Edward Villella, one of the top male dancers of the twentieth century and a former welterweight boxing champion, when he concluded that it took as much physical strength to dance a three-minute *pas de deux* as it did to go a three-minute round of boxing. Of course, there are differences. A boxer can grunt, sweat, frown, bleed, fall down, and generally let the audience witness his effort. A ballet dancer, however, has to pull off similar feats of strength and agility while smiling and seeming to fly through the air gracefully and effortlessly.

TURNOUT, THE FIVE POSITIONS AND THE VOCABULARY OF STEPS

The basis of ballet, and its primary difference from all other forms of dance, is what dancers call *turnout*: the positioning of the legs and feet in a 180-degree line at all times. In other words, instead of standing normally with the feet facing forward, they are "turned out" into a straight line with the toes pointing away from each other. Turnout begins in the hip socket, so that the knees as well as the toes face outward. It takes many years of practice to develop.

Not only must ballet dancers keep their feet and legs constantly turned out, but they must also begin and end each step from one of five basic positions, conveniently labeled first, second, third, fourth, and fifth position.

Moreover, the movements a dancer performs onstage (and in class as well) are—at least in strictly classical ballet—limited to a few hundred specific steps that were invented centuries ago in France and have been passed down from teacher to pupil through the years. Because there are only so many words in the English language, a speaker cannot simply invent words. Similarly, a ballet dancer cannot just invent a step. He or she must use the existing steps and perform them according to established standards that, depending on the particular teacher or *choreographer*, can be quite precise. This goes for every movement performed with legs, arms, and torso, right down to the tilt of the head and the angle of each finger.

To make things even more complicated, all the steps are still in French. This holds true whether the ballet class is being held in China, Russia, Africa, or Spain. When the teacher or choreographer says *plié*, the dancer bends his or her knees. When *relevé* is uttered, dancers springs up on their toes. Hearing *jeté*, the dancer leaps forward. This repertoire of French steps is just one of the aspects that have made ballet seem a little rigid, old-fashioned art not easily understood or appreciated by the average person.

THE RIGORS OF BALLET TRAINING

When considering turnout, the positions of the feet and the fixed set of steps that comprise the foundation of ballet, it is not hard to imagine the kind of training it takes to become a professional ballet dancer. Both genders, but especially females—who must learn to dance *en pointe,* or on the tips of their toes—begin ballet classes by age ten because it takes many years to mold the body into the unnatural shapes ballet demands.

Many parents send their children to ballet class as a

Many children take ballet lessons at a young age. While few pursue ballet on a professional level, there are many benefits from having a foundation in ballet, including grace, poise and flexibility, as well as an appreciation for music and the arts.

hobby, and for most it ends there, perhaps culminating in a role in an annual production of *The Nutcracker.* Even so, some ballet training during childhood yields many benefits, including poise, increased flexibility that can last well into adulthood, physical confidence, and often a lifelong appreciation of music and other performing arts.

Some of these students—those who possess inborn talent, a good physique, and a passion for ballet—will end up taking more and more classes. The few who are serious about becoming professionals will go on to audition at a prestigious ballet school, many of which are affiliated with ballet companies, or at a performing arts high school that focuses as much on dance as it does on academics.

From these schools, many dancers are then picked to join professional ballet companies, some as young as 17. Others major in dance at four-year colleges before auditioning for companies. The dancers who make it to this level have typically been training for at least ten years; if they are female they have been *en pointe* since about age 12. Most of them will need the preferred ballet physique: average height with long, lean limbs and muscles that are well defined but not bulky.

Once a dancer joins a professional company, the real work begins. An average schedule might include an hour-and-a-half morning class, a few hours of rehearsal, an afternoon class, some physical therapy if there are injuries to work on, and other forms of strength training such as Pilates or Nautilus. If the company is currently in performance, the day also includes either a matinee or nighttime performance. Most professional dancers work about 12 hours a day, six days a week.

Not surprisingly, ballet careers rarely extend far past the age of 40. By then a dancer's strength and agility are declining, though in relation to the general population the dancer is still amazingly strong and flexible. At this point some

(continued on page 20)

THE NUTCRACKER

Choreography by Lev Ivanov, 1892

Music by Pyotr Illyich Tchaikovsky

The most popular and well-known ballet in the United States is based on a nineteenth-century German fairy tale, "The Nutcracker and the Mouse King," by E.T.A. Hoffman. The two-act ballet begins at Christmastime in the home of Dr. and Mrs. Stahlbaum, who are hosting a holiday party. As elegantly dressed couples arrive with their children, we meet the Stahlbaums' daughter, Clara (in some productions called Marie), the story's protagonist. A charming and dreamy girl, Clara is elated when her godfather, the mysterious toy maker Drosselmeyer, appears in his black cape. Drosselmeyer enchants the children with life-sized dancing "toys" and then presents Clara, his favorite, with her Christmas gift: a soldier-like Nutcracker doll, which Clara adores but which, unfortunately, falls into the hands of her mischievous brother Fritz, who promptly breaks it and receives a scolding. After Drosselmeyer bandages the "wounded" doll and consoles Clara, the party disperses and darkness descends on the Stahlbaum house.

But Clara soon returns to the stage in her nightdress, searching for her Nutcracker under the Christmas tree and drifting off to sleep with the doll in her arms as the clock strikes midnight. Now Clara's dream begins to unfold onstage. Huge mice scurry in, terrifying her, and close on their heels comes their leader, the evil Mouse King. As Tchaikovsky's music increases in tempo and volume, the furniture in the room flies away and the Christmas tree grows to a gigantic height (special effects that generally delight the children in the audience). The Nutcracker comes to life and with him so do an entire army of toy soldiers, who fend off the mice while the Nutcracker duels the Mouse King. Just when it seem the Nutcracker will be defeated, Clara throws her shoe at the Mouse King, distracting him long enough for the Nutcracker to make the kill.

Again the scene changes and Clara finds herself alone with the Nutcracker, who has magically come to life in the form of a young prince. He leads her on a journey through the Kingdom of the Snow, where snowflakes (the corps de ballet dressed in white tutus) begin dancing around them along with the Snow Queen and King. Here the mood changes dramatically from a character-driven story ballet with much pantomime to a more classical dance-centered work. The Snow Queen and King perform a lyrical and dramatic pas de deux which closes the first act as Clara and her Nutcracker prince make their way onward to the Kingdom of Sweets.

Act II opens in this kingdom, a candyland of sorts reigned over by the Sugarplum Fairy—the ballet's star. At her command, a host of delicacies—chocolate from Spain, tea from China, coffee from Arabia and several others—come forward one by one to dance for the young travelers in a series of ethnically flavored divertissements. At the culmination, the Sugar Plum Fairy dances a grand pas de deux with her cavalier, then the Kingdom's inhabitants wave goodbye to Clara and the Nutcracker as they continue their journey—usually disappearing into the sky in a balloon.

The Nutcracker's appeal can perhaps be explained by the fact that it can be enjoyed on so many levels. Its fairytale quality, the liveliness of Act I and the short varietal dances in Act II make it a favorite of children, who stand in line by the thousands each fall to audition for regional productions across the country. Its music, including the "Waltz of the Flowers" and the "Dance of the Sugarplum Fairy," stands on its own as favorite Christmas music, and for serious balletgoers, it also presents lovely group and solo dances throughout the second act and in the Kingdom of the Snow.

(continued from page 17)
dancers retire, but most go on to become teachers and chore-ographers in their own right, training the next generation of students. For unlike other performing arts such as music, opera and theater, ballet's standards and repertoire are, by and large, not written down. Instead, they are passed down orally from teacher to students. Thus, great teachers and choreographers are highly revered in the ballet world and considered as important as, or even more important than, the dancers themselves.

WHAT IS IT ALL ABOUT?

One might wonder why dancers devote themselves to such a regimen. Unlike many musicians, actors, and singers, ballet dancers never earn much money, and their careers are fairly short. A dancer in his prime is much like an Olympic athlete in constant training—there is not much time for a social life, a family, or outside interests.

Obviously, ballet dancers share the same dedication to their art as do painters, poets, and composers. Its difficulty only makes it more of a challenge and a greater achievement once a dance or a role is mastered. Ballet is more than just physical prowess and athleticism because its main goal is not simply to jump high or spin quickly, but to communicate an emotion or idea and to do so with undeniable beauty.

That is what turnout is all about. It is not just an arbitrary quirk that somehow caught on and has been passed down to today's dancers. Turnout allows the dancer to move his lower body in much more varied ways, especially from side to side on stage, while providing the audience with a profile view of his legs and feet. Its angularity bestows a rarefied, crystalline look.

Beauty, and a certain dignity of form, are also at the root of ballet's vocabulary of steps, most of which portray either long, straight lines extending high and away from the

The drawing *Ballerina Standing at Bar* by **Edgar Degas** shows *turnout*, the technique employed by ballet dancers where the legs and feet form a 180-degree line at all times, and the toes of each foot are turned away from the other.

body, as in *arabesque*; graceful arcs and circles, as in *attitude* and *pirouette*; or the illusion of flight, as in *grand jeté* and *bourée*. These patterns are inherently symmetrical and visually pleasing, even to the untrained eye.

All of these steps are like the colors on an artist's palette. Choreographers "paint" the steps onto the dancers to create a kind of moving canvas. Not only are the dancers the medium, but they are also the artist—each with his own unique skills, personality, and expression. Ballet has been likened to sculpture or poetry that is actually alive with movement.

Then there is the music, an integral element of ballet—so integral, in fact, that the great choreographer George Balanchine defined ballet simply as "music personified." Ballet dancers, choreographers and admirers are usually music lovers, and if they do not start out that way, they certainly will acquire a deep appreciation of music gained by the added dimension of "dancing out the score," whether it be an orchestral symphony, a modern composition, or even pop or rock music.

The subject matter of most ballets, too, heightens the emotions of both performers and audiences. The first ballets portrayed ancient gods and myths; later, many romantic ballets were based either on classic tales such as *The Sleeping Beauty* and *Romeo and Juliet* or on spiritual topics such as death, the afterlife, and forgiveness. Today ballets deal with every subject imaginable—from primal experiences like love, longing, and sexuality to community, political, and social statements about racism, violence, and war. The combination of music, movements, and nonverbal acting creates a deeply emotional experience. Performing or watching a ballet often brings feelings of catharsis, sadness, and joy—sometimes all at once. The dancers' finely honed technique and almost superhuman athleticism only add to the experience.

As the dancer Mikhail Baryshnikov put it, ballet "has to do with the great blessings and disasters that are the center of our lives, the things one is usually too embarrassed or too frightened to talk about. There they were, in crystallized form."[1]

2

Ballet Begins
in Europe

When discussing the history of ballet, one must be sure to distinguish between social and folk dancing, which has existed in cultures throughout the world for thousands of years, and theatrical dancing, in which dancers perform for an audience. Early ballet was certainly influenced by the social dancing of its day—what would normally be called ballroom dancing. Although it often borrows ideas and movements from various folk dances, ballet is in essence a very specific kind of theatrical dancing.

The first seed of theatrical dancing was planted in ancient Greece, where song-and-dance celebrations in honor of the god Dionysus were part of Greek theater. The root of our word orchestra is the Greek *orkestra*, which means "round dancing floor." The nine Muses—the goddesses who inspired artists of all kinds and are the root of our word "music"—included Terpsichore, muse of poetry and dance.

A drawing of the Theater of Dionysus in Athens, Greece. Theatrical dancing is thought to have originated in ancient Greece, especially with the celebrations honoring the Greek god Dionysus that featured songs and dancing.

During the Dark and Middle Ages (about 410–1300 A.D.), theater—along with many of the other arts and sciences in Europe—went into a period of stagnation as the Catholic Church rose to prominence and people became more concerned with survival in this world and salvation in the next. The Renaissance of the fifteenth and sixteenth centuries brought an awakening of interest in all things human and especially in reviving the arts of the ancient Greeks and Romans. This is when ballet was born.

THE EARLIEST COURT BALLETS

Ballet comes from the Italian word *balla*, meaning dance, and in the Italian city-states of the fifteenth century, many *balli* (dances) were held. The aristocrats had the time and money to pursue and fund artistic endeavors. They hired dance teachers to instruct members of the court in the popular dances of the day, which were customary at the many galas thrown by the aristocracy—parties, weddings, and celebrations of all kinds. These *balli* or court dances involved very specific steps but

LE BALLET COMIQUE DE LA REINE (THE QUEEN'S BALLET SPECTACLE)

Choreography by Balthasar de Beaujoyeulx, 1581

Though generally regarded as the first court ballet, *Le Ballet Comique de la Reine* looked nothing like what we call ballet today. Firstly, it was performed not on a proscenium stage but on the floor of a huge hall of France's royal palace, with the public sitting in two levels of galleries looking down on the action. Secondly, it included not only dances but sung and spoken verses—as well as opulent scenery such as chariots, floats and fountains—a sort of cross between ballet, opera and theater. Thirdly, the dancers were not trained professionals but amateur nobles, and all male. *La Ballet Comique*—whose name does not imply a comical tone but rather a coherent dramatic theme, which preceding court spectacles had lacked—was staged during the reign of King Henri III (Catherine de Medici's son) and his wife, Queen Louise, to celebrate the marriage of Louise's sister, Margaret of Lorraine, to the Duc de Joyeuse. As was common back then, the marriage had a political purpose, to restore peace and strengthen the royal family's authority after many years of religious civil wars.

The ballet's plot managed to pay homage to the sovereign

looked more like what would now be called ballroom dancing. Their patterns resembled those of today's figure skaters who trace circles and arcs across a large floor.

A new form of dance called *entrées* materialized in the late 1400s. Today, we think of entrées as the courses of a meal, and that is just how these dances were "served up" to their royal audiences, usually between the courses of a long meal at wedding banquets. They were short dance segments, or *divertissements*, performed solely by men wearing wigs,

while employing classical Greek symbolism, which was much in vogue at the time thanks to the European Renaissance. The main characters were Ulysses, the hero of Homer's *Odyssey*, and Circe, the sorceress who holds him hostage. With the king and queen seated front and center of the action, the ballet made them into passive but central characters in the plot, which begins when Ulysses throws himself at the foot of the king in an effort to escape Circe, begging the king to summon Peace and Harmony in order to free him from the evil witch. For the next five hours, all manner of mythological characters of the sea— sirens, tritons, naiads—sing, recite and dance in intricate geometrical patterns such as squares, triangles and circles, which themselves were thought to be symbolic and even magical. In the end, Ulysses finds that he cannot break free of Circe, who controls the cycle of the seasons and is after all a supernatural being. He must appeal to the gods Pan, Mercury and Jupiter, who attack Circe's castle and take her prisoner. The ballet concludes with the goddess Athena paying honor to the Queen. The performers then presented the royals with symbolic emblems.

masks, and intricate costumes. They incorporated both poetry and singing into the dancing. To get an idea of how elaborately and seriously planned these entertainments could be, their décor, costumes, and stage machinery were often provided by the best artists of the time, including Leonardo Da Vinci for instance.

When the Italian noblewoman Catherine d'Medici married into the royal family of France in 1533, she brought knowledge of the *balli* with her to the French royal court. Catherine was a great admirer of dance and a famous hostess as well. To celebrate a family member's marriage in 1581, she presented the exorbitant *Le Ballet Comique de la Reine (The Queen's Ballet Spectacle)*, a six-hour extravaganza of music, song, and dance that is known as the first ballet, or "court ballet" as it was called back then.

Many of the early court ballets were based on gods, goddesses, and classic myths; ordinary people and problems were seen as crude and below the realm of high art. *Le Ballet Comique de la Reine*, for example, played out scenes from the legendary Greek story of Ulysses escaping from the sorceress Circe as told in Homer's *Odyssey*. The term "comique" actually does not mean that the ballet was meant to be comedic or funny; a closer translation would be "theatrical" or "dramatic."

BALLET'S FOUNDING FATHERS: BEAUCHAMPS, LULLY, AND NOVERRE

Ballet got a big boost when Louis XIV ascended to the throne of France. The young king had been schooled in all the courtly arts such as fencing and music, but dance was arguably his favorite. At age 15 he danced the role of the Apollo, the ancient Greek god of the sun, in *La Ballet de la Nuit (Ballet of the Night)*, which bestowed on him the popular title of "Sun King" for the rest of his life.

Louis XIV took the art of dance seriously, establishing the Academie Royale de Danse in 1661, which employed 13 ballet

LA BALLET DE LA NUIT (BALLET OF THE NIGHT)

Just as *Le Ballet Comique de la Reine* had at its core a political message to bear regarding the strengthening of the royal crown after a period of upheaval, so too did *La Ballet de la Nuit*. The five years prior to its debut had seen a series of outbreaks against the royal family perpetrated by France's judicial body, other nobles and the middle class and peasantry as well. By 1653 the monarchy had regained control and were eager to retain it by publicizing the teenage king in as grand a light as possible.

Fortunately, 15-year-old Louis was a talented and enthusiastic dancer. In *La Ballet de la Nuit*, a protracted ballet set on a proscenium stage with 43 separate dances spanning into the wee hours of the morning, he danced as several characters. The ballet takes as its subject the 12 hours of night beginning at 6 P.M. and ending at 6 A.M. or dawn. Its four scenes follow the course of the night: 6–9 P.M.; 9 P.M.–midnight; midnight–3 A.M.; and 3 a.m.–sunrise. During the first scene, early evening, the sun sets and characters such as bandits, gypsies and vagabonds appear in a darkened, lawless quarter of the city. The second scene portrays the time of night reserved for fetes and ballets, featuring masquerades and pantomimes. The third scene brings out Egyptian astrologers and the Persian priest Zoroaster, who are enchanted by the moon; when it goes into eclipse the theme turns darker as thieves loot a burning house while families flee the fire. In the final scene, darkness gives way to dawn as Aurora appears with her 12 hours of day. Here Louis made his entrance as Apollo, god of the sun, the bringer of light, riches, victory and peace. In a Roman-cut suit and headdress decorated in gilded "rays," Louis became known as the Sun King from then on.

Louis XIV of France, also known as the "Sun King," was a dance enthusiast and performer himself. He established the Academie Royale de Danse, and one of its 13 ballet masters, Pierre Beauchamps, would pioneer the five turnout positions and other basic steps still performed in ballet today.

masters—high-ranking teachers and choreographers. One of these was Pierre Beauchamps, who would go on to codify the five turned-out positions of the feet as well as many of the basic ballet steps still performed and still spoken solely in French today. Though even social or ballroom dancing favored a slight turnout to the feet, the development of the proscenium arch—the arch defining the front of a stage which separates the space between audience and performer—made turnout even more pronounced and important.

Early *balli* and court ballets in France were performed in ballrooms, or what today would be called "in the round." Dancers sometimes performed on raised platforms and could often be viewed from many angles. When the Paris Opera stage changed from a palace ballroom to a proscenium arch in 1669, the relationship between dancer and audience underwent an historic shift. Now the audience could only view the dancer from one angle—the front—while he moved primarily from one side of the stage to the other. Turnout provided the best way to achieve this side-to-side movement and give the audience a profile view of his legs and feet, all while he was facing them.

Louis XIV also hired violinist, composer, and dancer Jean-Baptiste Lully as director of the Acadamie Royale de Musique, within which Lully established his own dance academy. Today it is known as the Paris Opera Ballet, the oldest ballet academy in the world. From this academy, or *école de danse*, comes today's term *danse d'école*, or "dance of the school," meaning any dancing that honors the strict inventions and steps established for ballet during this time.

Another of ballet's founding fathers was Jean-Georges Noverre, also known as the "Shakespeare of dance." Instead of the court ballets that featured the aristocracy in elaborate, restrictive costumes, high heels, wigs, and masks, Noverre argued for a new kind of ballet that was more expressive and natural. He developed what is called the *ballet d'action*, the first kind of ballet to discard the use of songs or words and to depend entirely on dance, gesture, and pantomime set to music. Instead of short divertissements that could vary from subject to subject, the ballet d'action had a more coherent theme or plot. Noverre also encouraged dancers to discard their masks and lighten their costumes.

Noverre's ideas began to take root as he helped spread ballet through Europe. His career as a ballet master took him to Germany, England, Vienna, and Italy throughout the 1700s. His *Lettres sur la Danse et sur les Ballets (Letters on Dancing)* is one of the founding treatises on ballet, outlining his theories of ballet d'action—namely, that dance and dance alone could be its own art form and sustain drama, narrative,

LA FILLE MAL GARDÉE (THE ILL-WATCHED DAUGHTER)

Original choreography by Jean Dauberval, 1789; restaged by Frederick Ashton, 1960

Music by Ferdinand Herold

The first ballet d'action to portray the lives and concerns of ordinary people as opposed to gods and goddesses, *La Fille* is the oldest ballet currently performed in the world. Set in the countryside of France, it tells the story of Lise, a young girl in love with the handsome, devoted Colas. The only problem is that Lise's mother, the Widow Simone, wants her to marry Alain, the simpleton son of a wealthy landowner. Though Lise keeps sneaking off to steal moments with her beau, Simone is never far behind, ready to yank her daughter back into the house at every turn. Full of playful innocence and comedic touches, *La Fille*'s popularity rests on its bucolic setting, its charming mime sequences, its pastoral group dances, and most of all on the chemistry and dancing of its male and female leads, which must portray ardent young love without ever reaching into the territory of passion or sexuality (à la *Romeo and Juliet*). Ribbons are used as a symbol of love throughout the ballet.

and emotion. With Noverre's help, in due course, the new art form began to be practiced by devoted professionals instead of aristocratic amateurs whose main goal was to throw a memorable party.

WOMEN, COMMONERS, AND DEMOCRACY

In its first few centuries, ballet remained an art completely dominated by men. Then in 1681, Lully brought the first female dancer, known only as Mademoiselle Lafontaine, to the Paris

One of its highlights is a dance in which Lise and Colas intertwine themselves in a ribbon, spooling toward and away from each other and weaving the material into patterns between them. In another dance, Lise's girlfriends encircle and hold her en pointe via eight ribbons she holds above her head while they form a "wheel" around her, rotating her by moving the circle while each holding the end of one ribbon. The ballet also includes folkloric touches in the form of a clog dance, a maypole dance, and a morris dance (an English folk dance for men). Herold's score is by turns lively and lyrical, and there is some serious technical dancing for the two leads, who each perform precise feats of *batterie* (leg beats in the air) and some stunning turns as well as lovely, graceful *adagios* (slow, lyrical dances).

In the end, of course, Simone gives her approval and Lise and Colas are allowed to marry; this sets the whole happy village into a finale in which the lovers are celebrated. *La Fille* is the ballet version of an entertaining sitcom or a "chick flick"—light, romantic, and entertaining.

Marie Camargo, a very technical dancer who exemplified ballet's athleticism, was one of the premier ballerinas of the late 1600s. She also caused a stir among audiences when she would perform with shortened skirts (above her ankle) in order to draw attention to her footwork.

stage in *Le Triomphe de l'Amour (The Triumph of Love)*. Though little is known of Lafontaine's life or training, her appearance made history, and with the arrival of the ballerina there was no turning back—changes were underway.

As women began dancing in public, the costuming became more naturalistic and less confining, with the high heels of the court shed for soft, heelless slippers. Two of the first ballerinas were Marie Camargo, a *virtuoso* who dazzled audiences with her athleticism, and Maria Sallé, a more expressive and poetic dancer. The two women joined in ballet's first great rivalry, one that illustrated two aspects of dance—the technical versus the lyrical—that are still somewhat in competition today. Camargo scandalized the public by shortening her skirts' hemlines to above the ankle in order to show off her intricate footwork. Sallé did her bit to move things forward by abandoning the huge hoop skirts and wigs of the day for a muslin tunic, sandals, and her own loosened hair.

Around this time England, which had been putting on its own court ballets since the early 1600s, joined France and Italy in the ballet craze when Sallé went to London in 1733 to perform *Pygmalion*, depicting a statue brought to life by the Greek goddess Aphrodite. Ballet also took root in Russia when its empress, Anna Ivanovna, established the world's second ballet academy, the Imperial St. Petersburg School, in 1738. Though its name would change through the ages, becoming the Imperial Russian Ballet and later the Kirov Ballet, this very school still produces many of the world's leading dancers today.

As will be seen in subsequent chapters, ballet's history often coincided with the political currents of the countries in which it developed. So it was that in the late 1700s on the eve of the French Revolution that would overthrow France's royal house and establish a democracy in its place, ballet also began to illustrate this shift. Instead of taking the ancient gods or the splendor of the aristocracy for its subject matter, ballet began to focus more on common themes, ordinary characters, and natural settings. The year 1789 brought *La Fille Mal Gardée* (*The Ill-Watched Daughter*) to the stage, which told a quaint story about the lives and loves of French peasants living in the countryside. It became wildly popular and has become the oldest ballet that is still regularly performed today.

Even though commoners who were becoming skilled professionals took up the ballet, and even though its themes began to revolve around ordinary life, it is easy to see that the refinement and sophistication of Europe's royal courts forever marked ballet at its conception. The delicacy and dignity that still make ballet seem to many a "high art" are a legacy of the French and Italian aristocrats who gave ballet its start.

3

The Romantic Period

WOMEN *EN POINTE*

By the early 1800s, art and literature's romantic periods were well underway. The Romantics glorified humankind's emotional and spiritual dimensions while spurning the strictly scientific and intellectual view of the world, which they regarded as cold and inhuman. The effects were felt in the dance world and, combined with a few other coincidences, led to a full flowering of ballet's own great romantic period.

The first important event is the appearance on the scene of Italian-born ballerina Marie Taglioni. Her father Filippo, who was a ballet teacher, constructed the first romantic ballet, *La Sylphide*, especially to showcase his daughter's talents. The story of a nymph (a female spirit of the woods, which would go on to become a staple character in many ballets) who lures a young Scotsman away from his daily life and into the forest, *La Sylphide* marks several turning points in ballet.

Maria Taglioni, the daughter of ballet master Filippo Taglioni, danced in the first romantic ballet, *La Sylphide*, which was constructed by her father specifically for her. This ballet was groundbreaking in many ways, including the use of *corps de ballet* and *en pointe* dancing.

These milestones included the emergence of a large female *corps de ballet* backing up the lead ballerina, the lightening of the standard feminine costume to a long tulle skirt, the focus on naturalistic and spiritual topics, and, most importantly, the beginning of dancing en pointe. Pointe dancing, as much as turnout and the five positions, exemplifies ballet and is now the standard for all ballerinas. At the time of its introduction, however, audiences were enthralled to see Taglioni balancing on her tiptoes for long periods of time, not only because of the physical demands it ensued but also by the ethereal, lyrical quality it brought to the stage, presenting an image of Taglioni almost ready to lift off into flight.

Today, *pointe shoes* (or *toe shoes* as they are often called) are blocked—that is, the area surrounding the toes is greatly stiffened with extra material and glue beneath its shiny satin exterior. Ballerinas sometimes use soft padding or lambs' wool inside their shoes to cushion the effect of the toes hitting the floor repeatedly. Even so, a look at any ballerina's foot makes clear the strains of pointe dancing; the toes are frequently bruised and blistered, toenails often blackened or missing—a far cry from the dainty view of the shoed foot seen by the audience.

In Taglioni's time, however, the modern point shoe had not been invented, so the only support slippers provided came from darning their toes to reinforce and thicken the material there, making her achievement all the more impressive. For a time, French choreographer Charles-Louis Didelot helped his ballerinas balance on their toes—as well as fly through the air—with the aid of stage machines that hooked the dancers to wires. By the time of *La Sylphide*, Taglioni was balancing on her toes unaided by props.

If Taglioni was the first great prima ballerina, the second one followed closely on her heels—or toes. While "La Taglioni" was whisping across stages in her flowing white skirt, Fanny Elssler was displaying another strain of romanticism in Paris in *La Diable Boiteux* (*The Devil on Two Sticks*). Set in Spain, the ballet featured Elssler doing her *cachuca*, a balletic rendition of a traditional stomping, passionate Spanish dance featuring castanets. Comparisons between the earthy, sensual Elssler and the heavenly, refined Taglioni soon

The corps de ballet (shown here in *Swan Lake*) dance in unison behind the soloist, and can create a dazzling sight. No dancer stands out, as every single one of them is moving exactly the same way, with exquisite timing and precision.

became the talk of Europe, and ballet's second great female rivalry was born.

In more technical terms, the two ballerinas embodied two very different but essential characteristics of ballet. Taglioni displayed exemplary *ballon*—the ability to jump seemingly with ease and, for a moment, to even hover in the air. A modern (though not balletic) example of someone with terrific *ballon* is basketball star Michael Jordan. Elssler, on the other hand, perfected the art of *terre à terre*—a dance in which the feet barely leave the ground but which still expresses a fiery, sexy appeal.

THE *CORPS DE BALLET*

It was not only the great soloists who emerged into the spotlight during the romantic era. Ballets such as *La Sylphide*, and later *Giselle*, *La Bayadere*, and *Swan Lake*, all feature climactic scenes in which the lead male is lured into a mystical kingdom—be it a forest, a midnight lake or some sort of underworld—where he confronts his mistress among her kind, a large group of women who are not fully human. These "ballet blancs," as they were called because of the sheer white (*blanc* in French) costumes worn by the women, were the first to showcase an integral part of classical ballet: the *corps de ballet*, the

GISELLE

Original Choreography by Jules Perrot and Jean Coralli, 1841; restaged by Marius Petipa, 1884

Music by Adolphe Adam

G iselle is the quintessential romantic ballet in both its theme—which centers on the physical world versus the afterlife, and on revenge versus forgiveness—and in its look, which gives us long white tulle skirts (as opposed to the more modern short *tutus*) and a "ballet blanc" for a second act. Giselle is a role that requires great dramatic skill as well as virtuosic dancing for its lead ballerina; Carlotta Grisi made the role famous at the 1841 premiere of the ballet, and today it is requisite dancing for any ballerina worth her mettle.

The story is set in a Germanic village where the maiden Giselle lives with her mother. Though frail, Giselle loves to dance, and Act I features many lovely displays of her skill. When a nobleman, Count Albrecht, enters the village disguised as a peasant, he and Giselle fall in love. Following the tradition of many great ballets, operas and plays, it is love at first sight and soon Albrecht has sworn himself to Giselle. A hunting party of other nobles—among them Albrecht's friends and actual fiancé Bathilde—appear, and Albrecht's ruse is unmasked. Giselle, betrayed and wracked with grief, disintegrates into a famous "mad scene" which has her tearing at her hair, nearly company's crew of female dancers whose function was to dance in unison behind the soloist.

While a prima ballerina exults the audience with feats of balance, multiple turns, and high leaps, it is the corps' job to form a vision of lyrical harmony, with every arm moving at exactly the same angle and every leg pointed in exactly the same direction. In the best corps de ballets, no one dancer stands out

stabbing herself, and finally collapsing into the arms of her mother, dead.

Act II opens on a dark forest where Giselle is buried. Soon female spirits called Wilis, veiled and dressed in white, appear in a mournful promenade of hauntingly identical arabesques. Based on Slavonic folklore regarding vampire-like, dancing female spirits, the Wilis are the ghosts of women who have died before their wedding day, and they will kill any man who crosses their path by forcing him to dance to death. Giselle has become a Wili, and when a bereaved Albrecht comes to visit at her grave, the couple reunites in a series of melancholy, lyrical adagios, and pas de deuxes full of high lifts and controlled balances. Myrtha, the Wilis' queen, tries to force Albrecht to dance to his death, but Giselle interferes, distracting Myrtha and at times dancing in place of Albrecht, until dawn breaks and the Wilis retreat to their graves. Though Giselle's spirit disappears along with her sisters, Albrecht has been saved by her act of forgiveness. In addition to the intensely emotional mad scene and the partnered dancing in Act II, the harmonious corps dances of the Wilis, bodies bent forward and legs all lifted to the same height straight back in arabesque, are another highlight of this unabashedly romantic (in every sense of the word) ballet.

either physically or technically. Their job is to blend into one harmonious whole; timing and control are their specialties.

Today's corps de ballets include both genders, and in some companies they are used as centerpieces in and of themselves, not only as a backdrop to the soloists. The ballet blanc sections of the romantic ballets, however, remain the realm of the female corps and often provide as many emotional and technical highlights as do the featured solos, albeit of a different kind. The "Dance of the Cygnets" in *Swan Lake* is a prime example of a group dance of amazing precision and timing; so too is the sight of dozens of dancers waving their arms gracefully in unison, creating a mesmerizing illusion of birds in flight.

PETIPA'S FORMULA FOR CLASSICAL BALLET
While the first production of *La Sylphide* took place in Paris and the most famous ballerinas of the day were still coming from Italy, the second half of the nineteenth century saw the axis of the ballet world shift from Western Europe to Russia. Yet it was a Frenchman who was largely responsible for this.

As the Grand Ballet Master of the Imperial Russian Ballet (nowadays known as the formidable Kirov Ballet), Marius Petipa created five of ballet's greatest classics in the late nineteenth century: *Don Quixote, La Bayadere, The Sleeping Beauty, Swan Lake,* and *The Nutcracker,* as well as restaging *Giselle* and *La Coppelia.*

All of Petipa's masterworks share common traits that mark them as the underpinnings of what is now regarded as the classical repertoire. For narratives, they take either the romantic idea of a man lured to an otherworld by a spirit-woman (as in *La Bayadere* and *Swan Lake*) or traditional works of literature and fairy tales (as in *Don Quixote, The Sleeping Beauty,* or *The Nutcracker*). They generally begin with group dances in a character or folkloric vein, with much pantomime used to put the story in motion, then proceed to a pivotal dream or ballet blanc sequence featuring the lead

The romantic ballet *Giselle* was restaged by Marius Petipa in 1884 and also features a stunning display of corps de ballet, as well as demanding the highest level of acting and dancing skills for the prima ballerina's role.

ballerina and her corps. The last act of the ballet usually culminates with a variety of dances not particularly tied to the plotline; the setting of these divertissements is often the wedding celebration of the hero and heroine, but in reality they are just artistic excuses to showcase the dancers' finesse with differing styles. Finally, the ballet climaxes with the *grand pas de deux*, a Petipa invention recognized as the ballet standard the world over.

The grand pas de deux, which translates simply as "big step for two," begins with an *adagio* (slow, lyrical dance) between the male and female dancer, marked by supported high *extensions* of the woman's legs, multiple *pirouettes* (a kind of one-legged spin) aided by the man's guiding hand above the woman's head or at her waist, and acrobatic lifts of the woman over the man's head. This is followed by an *allegro* (a quick, lively combination) by the male dancer showcasing his ability to leap and spin, an allegro for the ballerina featuring light footwork and pirouettes, and a *coda* (or finale) that reunites them in an exuberant flourish.

The dramatic action of the opening scenes, the corps' presentation of the dreamy ballet blancs, the divertissements showing a range of ethnically tinged styles, and the grand pas de deux are what audiences of classical ballet have come to expect in a full-length piece. Petipa put this formula in place and added the last necessary element: great music.

Up until Petipa's time, most ballet music was given only secondary consideration to the dancing. The Russian composer Pyotr Illyich Tchaikovsky changed that. By composing scores that were complex and symphonic as well as danceable, he added another dimension of beauty to the art. His scores for *Swan Lake, The Sleeping Beauty,* and *The Nutcracker* are famous compositions even for non-balletgoers. Tchaikovsky's music and Petipa's choreography brought ballet to new heights and secured Russia's place in the history of classical ballet.

THE THREE SCHOOLS OF CLASSICAL BALLET

Not only did the nineteenth century see the formulation of romantic classical ballet, but it was also during this time that three distinct styles, or schools, of ballet technique began to be recognized and consciously passed down through structured teaching systems, published books, and, as always, directly from teacher to student.

The French School, the oldest, was the original basis for ballet as developed in the court of Louis XIV by ballet masters such as Beauchamps and Noverre, as seen in the previous chapter. Known for its grace and elegance rather than its technical virtuosity, the French School was nevertheless held in high regard. While the Russians were soaking up every last detail of French technique under Petipa in the late nineteenth century, French ballet itself was undergoing a period of stagnation. During this time, Parisian audiences were entirely male, and they seemed much more interested in carousing with the all-female casts backstage than in watching them from the audience. Many famous paintings by Edgar Degas capture the look and feel of French ballet during this time.

The Italian School, known for its dexterity, difficulty of its steps, high leaps, and multiple turns, was largely the creation of Carlo Blasis, who became director of the Imperial Dancing Academy in Milan in 1837. Blasis did the ballet world a huge service when he wrote down all that was known about the dance's structure in two books, *An Elementary Treatise upon the Theory and Practice of the Art of Dancing* and *The Code of Terpsichore*. Blasis' technique was passed down through his pupil Giovanni Lepri to Enrico Cecchetti, a brilliant dancer, teacher, and mime artist who brought the athletic Italian style to Russia in 1887, where he stunned audiences and went on to become a legendary teacher. He developed his own regimented style of training involving very specific daily and weekly lesson

(continued on page 48)

SWAN LAKE

Choreography by Marius Petipa and Lev Ivanov, 1877

Music by Pyotr Illyich Tchaikovsky

Perhaps the most well-known and popular of the classical ballets, *Swan Lake* serves as an example of Marius Petipa's formula: an introductory group scene that sets the action in motion, a dream sequence or ballet blanc, and a culminating party scene or gathering of the original group of characters with several diver-tissements inserted for variety, crowned by a grand pas de deux. It is all set to the symphonic accompaniment of the great composer Tchaikovsky. *Swan Lake*'s female lead switches from a swan queen named Odette in Act II to an evil impersonator named Odile in Act III. The same ballerina dances both roles. It also continues past the third act with a short final act.

Based on a German folktale, the ballet's first act occurs in the court of Prince Siegfried. It is his birthday, and his mother the Queen presents him with the gift of a crossbow while reminding him that his time has come to choose a bride. Though he dances with several women, he remains distracted, even melancholy, and when the party leaves (after performing various group waltzes and a *pas de trios*, or "dance for three"), takes his crossbow to a nearby lake to hunt.

Act II opens on the moonlit lake where the prince sees swans flying and aims his crossbow. Suddenly, a swan is in front of him in the form of a woman-creature—Odette, the Swan Queen—who flutters her "wings" nervously. The evil magician Baron von Rothbart has cursed Odette. By day, she and her fellow maidens are swans; between midnight and dawn they resort to women, watched over by von Rothbart in the guise of an owl. The curse can only be broken by a man's sincere pledge of love. Among *Swan Lake*'s many charms are the flowing, birdlike movements of its star ballerina and corps, all dressed in white tutus and feathered head caps. The prince becomes enchanted with Odette and Act II sees their pas de deuxes alternating with group dances of the corps of swans.

One of the most breathtaking is the "Dance of the Cygnets" in which four of the swans, arms intertwined and hands linked, dance in quick, perfect unison. The prince, of course, declares his love to Odette before dawn breaks, and she and her fellow maidens revert to swans and "fly" off. Here one sees some of the commonalities among the romantic ballets: *Giselle*'s Wilis return to their graves at dawn, *Swan Lake*'s maidens return to bird form. Also the story turns on a man's vow, which holds the power to either destroy a woman or liberate her from a miserable destiny—themes that run through *Cinderella* and *The Sleeping Beauty* as well.

Act III returns to the royal court where Siegfried's mother again insists on his choosing a bride. For the betrothal festivities, dancers from Hungary, Poland, Spain, and Naples arrive—another of Petipa's formulas for showcasing a variety of national dances. Again Siegfried is unimpressed with the six women presented to him as potential brides, but when a mysterious nobleman (von Rothbart in disguise) arrives with his daughter Odile—danced by the same ballerina as Odette, but in a black tutu and acting much livelier and cunning—the prince takes her for his beloved swan maiden. Amid the already full festivities, they dance a grand pas deux whose coda culminates in Odile performing 32 *fouettés*— quick turns done from one leg with the other whipping in and out. Siegfried pledges his troth to Odile and in that moment von Rothbart reveals himself, victorious in his attempt to make the prince renounce his vow to Odette, who must now remain a swan forever.

Act IV returns to the lakeside where Odette is grieving her betrayal by Siegfried. When he comes to her, penitent, to confess his mistake, the two decide to end their lives together and thus free themselves to unite in the afterlife. Though von Rothbart tries to stop them, the two dive into the lake, which breaks the curse, while the swan maidens gather to bid farewell to their queen and her lover, who are seen sailing off into the afterlife as von Rothbart perishes.

Four "cygnets" during the "Dance of the Cygnets" in the second act of *Swan Lake*. Based on a German folktale, *Swan Lake* features characters who are swans by day and women by night. Their birdlike appearance is conveyed through the dancers' costumes and movements.

(continued from page 45)

plans, described in his book, *A Manual on the Theory and Practice of Classical Theatrical Dancing*. The book is used to this day—particularly in England, where he later settled—to produce dancers of great technical strength.

The Russian School is a synthesis of the two other schools: the French brought by Petipa and his forerunners and the Italian brought by Cecchetti. Thus many consider its combination of serene elegance and breathtaking virtuosity the most complete and well-developed technique in all of ballet. Near the close of the nineteenth century, young Russian dancers were begging to be trained by Cecchetti. Through him one can trace not only the best dancers of the early 1900s—Anna Pavlova, Vaslav Nijinsky, and Michael Fokine—but also many students who went on to develop companies or teaching systems of their own, such as Agrippina Vaganova in Russia and Ninette de Valois in England.

The early 1900s would see many of these magnificent dancers and teachers taking the Russian technique back to France and not only revitalizing ballet for the next century, but also spreading it from Europe throughout the world.

4

The Russians Bring Ballet to the World

DIAGHILEV'S BALLETS RUSSES

If ballet's progress in the nineteenth century was marked by French dance makers such as Petipa and the French School of ballet taking root on Russian soil, then the twentieth century brought just the opposite: native Russians who took their training and creative vision to France—and then to the world. Although Petipa and others before him had worked to bring structure and narrative clarity to the nineteenth century classics, the twentieth century began with a revolt against Petipa's classicism and a push for more natural, expressive ways of moving.

The modern ballet era began in 1909 in Paris when the Russian Serge Diaghilev—neither a dancer nor a choreographer but an arts enthusiast and impresario—debuted the Ballets Russes, a company whose influence, through the various choreographers and dancers it spawned, is still felt today. The

Russian dancer and choreographer Michael Fokine was one of the first to break away from Petipa's formulaic ballets based on fairy tales, as well as creating more prominent roles for male dancers. The Ballets Russes company, which also included figures such as George Balanchine and Vaslav Nijinsky, helped usher in the era of modern ballet.

history of the Ballets Russes reads like a roster of the greatest ballet figures of all time: Michael Fokine, Vaslav Nijinsky, Anna Pavlova, Ninette de Valois, and George Balanchine, all of whom did their part to both spread the existing art form worldwide and to modernize it. In addition to nurturing famous dancers and choreographers, Ballets Russes also became known for working with the premier artists and musicians of the time. Igor Stravinsky, Maurice Ravel, Claude Debussy, and Serge Prokoviev created scores for Ballets Russes, and artists such as Pablo Picasso, Henri Matisse, and Max Ernst devised sets.

One of Ballet Russes' most influential dancers and choreographers, Michael Fokine in particular rejected Petipa's formula for the multi-act classical ballet based on fairy tale and the afterlife; instead he created shorter ballets with more earthy, folkloric themes and more passionate choreography, such as *The Firebird, L'Spectre de la Rose* (*The Spirit of the Rose*), *Petrouchka,* and *Scheherazade.* His ballets also gave more stage time to the male dancers, something Paris audiences had greatly missed in the late nineteenth century when men had been relegated to sexually obsessed observers in the audience.

THE GREAT NIJINSKY AND LA PAVLOVA

One of these male dancers in particular made an indelible impression with his fierce sensuality and heretofore-unseen technical strength. Vaslav Nijinsky, the star of many of Fokine's ballets, could not only leap higher and beat his legs faster than anyone before him, but he projected such charisma that he immediately became Ballet Russes' biggest star. As the Spirit in *L'Spectre de la Rose,* Nijinsky's costume of flower petals and fluidly melting limbs made him seem more plantlike than human; as the puppet come to life in *Petrouchka,* his half-human melancholy was palpable. As the Golden Slave in *Scheherazade,* his erotic and highly physical dancing raised eyebrows. His emotional and technical range seemed unlimited.

Although Nijinsky was an enormously gifted dancer, he is perhaps best known for two ballets he choreographed which broke many dance and social barriers at the time. In

Composer Igor Stravinsky (left), shown here with dancer Vaslav Nijinsky, scored *Le Sacre du Printemps* (*The Rite of Spring*) for the Ballets Russes. The music and its accompanying choreography caused violent reactions with audiences, and the ballet closed after only seven performances.

1912's *L'Apres-midi d'un Faune* (*Afternoon of a Faun,* not to be confused with Jerome Robbins' 1953 ballet of the same name), Nijinsky took the flattened, angular poses seen in Greek art and used them to portray a primal scene come to life: a man-beast carousing with young nymphs of

LE SACRE DU PRINTEMPS (RITE OF SPRING)

Choreography by Vaslav Nijinksy, 1913

Music by Igor Stravinsky

ite of Spring, as it is commonly known even though Stravinsky himself called it "The Coronation of Spring," began with the composer's famous score, upon which Nijinsky's choreography was built. The music in and of itself—discordant, non-melodic and thunderous—brought about its own revolution in the way classical music was perceived and composed. But since both the score and the ballet premiered together on a May night in Paris in 1913, the effect on the audience's senses was doubled.

In two acts, *Rite of Spring* basically takes the viewer back to an imagined, prehistoric Russia—which in many minds played out as a metaphor for the darkness of the human subconscious. Act I opens on a green hillside at the end of winter. Young women and men, dressed in heavy peasant robes, dance in groups, first lightheartedly and then more aggressively. At one point the men carry the women offstage, playing at abducting them, until a wise tribal elder with a long beard and tall hat enters and the youngsters become still. The act ends with the men dancing a frenzied ritual of earth worship.

The second act opens on a harsher landscape marked with sacred stones and framed by ox skulls hanging from poles.

the forest. The sexual overtones and non-balletic movement of the piece caused scandal and sensation in Paris
audiences, but that was nothing compared to Nijinsky's
creation the following year: a joyful praise of Russia's
pagan history called *Le Sacre du Printemps* (*The Rite of Spring*).

A group of tribal virgins encircles the stage and performs
a magical dance, choosing one of their own as a sacrifice
in the process. The chosen woman stands alone in
the middle of the circle as the tribe gathers round her,
the ancestors are summoned, and the whole tribe dances
a violent, sacrificial rite until the chosen woman falls
dead on the ground.

As if the subject matter weren't controversial enough in
polite Paris society, Nijinsky's choreography—described as
asymmetric, spasmatic, sluggish, larvalike, ugly—shocked
audiences by presenting movements never before seen.
Instead of turnout, the dancers' feet were turned in with their
legs knock-kneed. One dancer commented that, instead of
aspiring to the lightness and grace typical of ballet, Nijinsky
actually constructed the dance so that every movement
actually caused physical pain, as if the dancers' bodies were
being thrown heavily around the stage. The audience didn't
quite know what to make of it all. Boos and jeers almost
drowned out the orchestra, men came to blows, and outside
the theater a riot erupted. Nijinsky, Stravinsky and Ballet Russes
impresario Serge Diaghilev were said to be despondent
afterward. The ballet disappeared from the repertoire after
just six more performances and was restaged 75 years later
by the Joffrey Ballet in 1988.

In this ballet—or anti-ballet as some might call it—dancers stomped heavily onstage as if engaged in a tribal rite celebrating the coming of spring. There were no pointe shoes, no delicate pirouettes, no chivalrous partnering: just a group of bodies moving pigeon-toed and animal-like to an ominous score by Igor Stravinsky, the climax of which portrayed the sacrifice of a virgin. Brazenly ahead of its time and much too shocking for audiences to support,

L'APRES-MIDI D'UN FAUNE (AFTERNOON OF A FAUN)

Choreography by Vaslav Nijinsky, 1912

Music by Claude Debussy

Nijinsky's first attempt at choreography, which shocked and scandalized Paris audiences, was ironically based on the strains of Debussy's *Prelude a' L'Apres-midi d'un Faune*, a soft, lulling piece of flute music which sounds more like the backdrop for an idyllic picnic than an erotically charged ballet that broke with nearly every tradition. Taking his cue from the music, Nijinsky's main character (danced by himself) is a faun—a half-human and half-animal creature of the woods much like a satyr or man-goat—who comes upon seven young nymphs in the forest. Unlike Debussy's gentle score, however, Nijinsky's faun is full of primal sexual energy as he attempts to mate with one of the nymphs, who drops a scarf as she flees from him. The ballet culminates with the faun alone, fondling her scarf and finally lying on top of it erotically, arching into a spasm of sexual delight. Not only did Nijinsky insert a sexual theme into what could have been an innocent pastoral interlude, his choreography also went in the opposite direction of ballet.

Taking his visual inspiration from the bas-relief of Greek

it played only seven performances and was not restaged until 75 years later.

Nijinsky's life was just as consuming offstage. He was Diaghilev's live-in lover for a time—an arrangement he claimed to have agreed to for the sake of his career and financial security. When he unexpectedly married while touring South America at the age of 24, Diaghilev was so furious he fired Nijinsky, an event that marked the beginning of Nijinsky's

friezes in which flattened characters stood in profile, Nijinsky gave *Faune* no toe shoes—indeed, not even a pointed foot—no delicate arcs or curves. The dancers move about a shallow portion of the stage by way of a bent-kneed, flat-footed shuffle, faces never looking at the audience but turning suddenly one way or another in profile with shoulders stiff, arms angled sharply, and hands molded shut with no space between the fingers. Surely ballet had never before, or ever since, seen anything quite like it. Though the nymphs do exude a certain feminine grace—with arms linked as they shuffle first right and then left, changing direction without cue from the music—the faun's movements are more animalistic as his feet paw at the floor and he arches his pelvis far forward in attempting to join with the desired nymph. With *Faune*, Nijinsky, perhaps without realizing it, created the first modern dance. Though Isadora Duncan was during this same period improvising the beginnings of naturalistic, modern dance onstage, she created no formal choreography to hand down. Even so, *Faune* is categorized as a ballet, albeit a very new kind of ballet that broke all the rules and widened the thematic and structural scope of dance in one giant leap.

descent into schizophrenia. In 1919, at the age of 30, he entered an institution and spent the rest of his life in mental hospitals throughout Europe. Unknowingly, his work had been a harbinger of the modern dance movement that would soon begin in the United States.

Another star of the Ballets Russes that shone just as brightly, but much less controversially, was Anna Pavlova, a young ballerina who had been trained by both Petipa and Cecchetti in Russia. In fact, Cecchetti had devoted three years of his career solely to her training. Lithe, willowy, and utterly poetic in her dancing, Pavlova captivated audiences first in Russia, then in Paris, and finally worldwide when she began to manage her own career—an unheard-of feat for a female dancer before that time.

From 1911 until 1929, Pavlova toured the world, performing solos and abbreviated versions of the classics in many countries that had never before seen ballet, including Australia, Japan, India, South America, North America, South Africa, and New Zealand, where ballet companies began springing up soon after her legendary appearances. Pavlova's signature piece was *The Dying Swan*, a one-act ballet created by Fokine in which the ballerina portrayed a dying bird. A filmed performance still survives, though it is not commercially available. "La Pavlova," as she was affectionately known, almost singlehandedly spread ballet from its roots in Europe and Russia to the entire world. Her achievement would be mirrored a few decades later by Margot Fonteyn, a ballerina from England, where Pavlova eventually made her home.

ENGLAND'S ROYAL BALLET AND MARGOT FONTEYN

Pavlova's tireless touring and the far-flung synergy of Ballet Russes are also indirectly responsible for the flourishing of the ballet movement in England. After the great ballet master Cecchetti worked with the company from 1909 to 1918, he moved to London where one of his pupils, former Ballets Russes dancer Ninette de Valois, was working to establish a ballet company that would eventually be known as Britain's Royal Ballet.

For a choreographer, de Valois chose Frederick Ashton, a native Ecuadorian (born William Mallandaine) who developed a passion for dancing after seeing Pavlova perform in Peru. Although de Valois' company's name changed from the Vic-Wells Ballet to the Sadler's Wells Ballet and finally to the Royal Ballet, Ashton remained its primary choreographer for 35 years, helping define a style of dancing known for its suppleness and interesting curves and angles in the upper body.

Ashton's muse was British ballerina Margot Fonteyn who had debuted at the Vic-Wells Ballet in 1935 at the tender age of 16. Though not an extremely athletic dancer, Fonteyn charmed audiences with her perfect balletic physique, pure and seemingly effortless *line*, regal beauty, and the warmth of her characterizations. Ashton created some of the Royal Ballet's masterpieces around her, such as the plotless *Symphonic Variations* and the story of the ethereal water sprite *Ondine*, as well as leading roles in many of the Royal Ballet's restagings of classics such as *The Sleeping Beauty*.

Fonteyn's stellar career in England was only half of her story; in the 1960s she would team up with the greatest male dancer in the world, and together they would help spawn a worldwide dance boom just as Pavlova had in the early 1900s.

THE SOVIET REVOLUTION YIELDS BALANCHINE AND MORE

As if nurturing the century's greatest European dancers and choreographers were not enough, Ballet Russes also contained the seed of America's ballet future in the form of a young dancer named Georgi Balanchivadze who left Soviet Russia in 1924 to join Diaghilev and his fellow dancers in Monte Carlo, where Ballet Russes had stationed itself after the Bolshevik Revolution of 1917.

Wealthy American ballet enthusiast Lincoln Kirstein (left) provided Balanchine with an opportunity to start his own ballet company in the United States after Diaghilev died in 1929, leading to the creation of the New York City Ballet.

As had happened before, international politics had far-reaching implications in ballet's history—namely, when czarist Russia became the Soviet Union, many of its dancers and choreographers fled under the strain of the new Socialist order. Ironically, the Communist Party actually lent its full support to ballet, funding it so generously that by mid-century, Moscow's Bolshoi Ballet would stun the world upon its first tour of the West. The "Russian Method" of instruction also went into full gear at this time under the auspices of Agrippina Vaganova. She was a student of Cecchetti's who remained in St. Petersburg (then Leningrad) after the revolution, merging the finer points of the French and Italian Schools into the "Vaganova system" as outlined in her book *Fundamentals of Classic Dance*.

When Balanchivadze arrived in France, Diaghilev quickly changed the young man's name to George Balanchine and asked him to begin choreographing new works for the troupe. This Balanchine did with great prolificness, creating eight ballets in as many years. Though he was trained as a dancer, it soon became clear that Balanchine's gift lay in choreography, and in 1928 he created *Apollo*, a portrayal of the life of the Greek sun god, and the first of many Balanchine classics. *Apollo* is actually touted as the first "neoclassical" ballet, as Balanchine's work would come to be known—keeping the purity and form of classical ballet but stripping it of its elaborate storylines, mime, and heavy theatrics, thus resulting in a leaner, cleaner kind of classicism.

Balanchine might have gone on to create many more works for Ballets Russes, but the company that had become the trunk of so many branches on the tree of ballet collapsed upon Diaghilev's death in 1929. While others went on to restructure the troupe, Balanchine went in search of a new company to call his own. He found his chance in 1933 when Lincoln Kirstein, a wealthy American heir and ballet lover, made him an offer to come to the United States and establish his own company. Balanchine agreed, and thus was born what would eventually become the New York City Ballet, where Balanchine's neo-classicism could take root and flower into a uniquely American strain of ballet.

5

The Balanchine Era

DANCE IN AMERICA

Where ballet is concerned, the United States is extremely lucky. The European art form with aristocratic beginnings had, for the most part, paid only occasional visits to America's shores. America proved to be a devoted audience as witnessed during Fanny Elssler's 1840 tour, when the Senate recessed to mark her first performance in Washington, D.C. While the United States had produced a few dancers, and had seen the creation of two professional companies in Philadelphia and San Francisco by the 1930s, the country undeniably entered ballet quite late in the game. When ballet did finally arrive with full force, anyone could have brought it over. Instead of just anyone, however, America got George Balanchine, arguably the greatest ballet master of the century—and, some say, of all time. Balanchine's benefactor, Lincoln Kirstein, adored ballet but knew very little about it. Thus Balanchine was

George Balanchine is considered to be one of ballet's greatest masters. With the help of Lincoln Kirstein, he founded the New York City Ballet in 1948 and showcased his own style of ballet, which eschewed plot and complexity and favored female dancers.

given free reign to create any kind of company he liked, and he ended up creating one quite different from anything that had existed before.

First came the school. In 1934 Balanchine founded the School of American Ballet and soon after created his first American work for its students—*Serenade*, a ballet without a story or a set, danced in simple costumes by a female ensemble to a Tchaikovsky symphony. The structure of

Serenade foreshadowed all of the elements that would come to mark Balanchine's work: his favoritism of the female dancer, his disregard for acting or too much plot, his sharp simplicity, and, most of all, his musicality. It remains one of the most widely performed and popular of his works.

After several attempts to start a professional company as well as stints working in Hollywood and on Broadway, Balanchine finally founded the New York City Ballet (NYCB) in 1948 and with it began establishing his vision of what American neoclassical dance should be.

 SERENADE

Choreography by George Balanchine, 1934

Music by Pyotr Illyich Tchaikovsky

The most popular and widely performed of Balanchine's ballets, *Serenade,* was created as a training exercise for his students in the year after he opened the School of American Ballet. "I wanted to teach them how to be onstage," he has said. It is considered the first plotless ballet and the beginning of Balanchine's brand of neo-classicism, showcasing his legendary musicality, symmetry, and speed. Danced in simple leotards and long tulle skirts, *Serenade* begins with the foundation of all classical ballet, a large corps of women moving in unison, then mutates into various smaller combinations.

Balanchine imbued the ballet with the happenstances of real rehearsals—a woman falls to the floor and, exhausted, stays there; another enters late—and also with a contemplation on relationships between the sexes as in a lovely, at times heart-breaking dance between one man and three women. Starting with *Serenade*, Balanchine began a trademark of constructing dances that simultaneously test the caliber of a company

THE WORLD ACCORDING TO MR. B

"Mr. B.," as his dancers affectionately called him, held strong opinions about dancing and dancers. Firstly, he greatly preferred the female to the male dancer, insisting that women were the core and the soul of ballet. Men existed to showcase them. Their bodies were naturally more flexible, and therefore their line was naturally more beautiful. Balanchine would famously declare, "Ballet is a woman."[1]

His views could at times seem obsessive. He preferred that his female dancers not marry, but he in fact married four ballerinas—Tamara Geva, Vera Zorina, Maria Tallchief, and

while extracting from the music tremendous emotion in the simplest gestures—an arm moving slowly to the forehead, two dozen women in identical arabesque, a woman's hand placed just so on a man's shoulder. The result is both a standard and an artistic expression of the highest order.

If a company has a weak spot, Balanchine's choreography will reveal it. Is the corps moving with perfect timing? How many fast *piques* (traveling moves up to pointe) can they do in a row? Can they all turn repeatedly without falling behind tempo? Balanchine's bias toward the female dancer is evident—only one man shows up onstage—and so is his belief in fostering a strong corps de ballet instead of exclusively nurturing only big names and stars. In *Serenade*, as in subsequent works of Balanchine, all the traditional rules of ballet are intact, accounted for, and even improved upon. As a whole, his dancers routinely had better extension, strength, and line than those that came before them, but those rules in his hands are stripped bare and made visible, with nothing extra coming between the dancer, the dance, and the audience.

Tanaquil LeClerq—and lived with Alexandra Danilova. When his favorite dancer, Suzanne Farrell—with whom he was rumored to be in love—married fellow NYCB dancer Paul Mejia, Balanchine reportedly cut Mejia's roles, forcing the couple to leave the company. Still, in addition to Farrell, Balanchine's training produced some of the best dancers of the century in Merrill Ashley, Patricia McBride, Allegra Kent and Kyra Nichols. His roster of great male students—Edward Villella, Jacques D'Amboise, and Peter Martins among them— proved that a dancer did not have to be his favorite in order to benefit from his tutelage.

As for physique, Balanchine preferred tall, long-limbed, long-necked dancers. He claimed there was more to see in a tall dancer—more line and extension. This preference, along with his Russian-bred technique, produced American dancing that was leaner, stronger, and crisper than any that had been seen before.

Balanchine also changed the historical role of the corps de ballet, negating the idea of a corps that exists only to perform ensembles as a backdrop for a soloist. His corps was the heart of his company from which his "stars" were eventually singled out and nurtured. He also eschewed strict uniformity of movement in the corps and urged his corps dancers to express themselves individually. However, his corps pieces are among the most harmoniously danced works on the stage.

In addition to his theories on the corps, Balanchine deplored the "star system" of Europe in which companies courted and hosted touring guest artists to dance in front of their corps. Instead, Balanchine wanted each of his dancers to train hard and aspire to the rank of soloist. Although obviously not all of them would make it, the stars Balanchine did feature came out of his own corps in a "promote from within" system.

Perhaps Mr. B's biggest contribution is the storyless

ballet. While he staged some reproductions of romantic classics such as *Don Quixote*, he much preferred ballets without a narrative. "How much story do you want?" he asked. "You put a man and woman onstage together, and already it's a story."[2] Instead of his choreography existing inside a fanciful narrative or fairy tale, it acts chiefly as a straightforward and simple showcase for virtuosic dancing set to symphonic music. For instance, *Agon* presents 12 dancers in practice clothes competing with each other. *The Four Temperaments* is simply a series of dances portraying one of the four medieval human temperaments—melancholic, sanguine, phlegmatic, and choleric—or, elementally speaking, earth, air, water, and fire.

Musicality is the last of Balanchine's hallmarks—connected, perhaps, to his early training as a pianist. Tying his steps closely to the score, his dances become almost balletic illustrations of the music with the simple scenery and costumes adding to the pared-down effect of a transparent vision of dance. The steps are not simply vehicles for expressing some imagined emotion but are the point of the piece and inherently contain the emotion themselves.

That is not to say that his ballets were not romantic or passionate; in fact, he believed that much of the passion of the dance came not from an overlaid story but from the intermingling of bodies themselves as they danced in groups, trios and duos. Balanchine's pas de deuxes can subtly imply an intensely romantic feeling, but this feeling arises naturally out of the choreography and not from a plot the audience reads in the program.

NYCB VERSUS ABT

While Balanchine was developing his neoclassical, no-star company in New York City, dancer Lucia Chase in 1937 had founded American Ballet Theatre (ABT) but a half-mile away. ABT was the United States' other great company, with

Ballerina Alicia Markova was one of many guest artists who danced with the American Ballet Theatre. Started by Lucia Chase in 1937, the ABT performed classic ballets and created new ones, touring the country instead of basing itself solely in one city.

a vision very different from Balanchine's. ABT focused equally on creating new ballets and restaging the great European classics such as *Giselle* and *La Bayadere* for American audiences. And instead of basing itself entirely in New York City, ABT became a touring company, taking its roster of Old World classics around the United States. Though it did eventually nurture its own generation of American dancers, it relied for stars more on touring European and Russian artists such as Alicia Markova, Anton Dolin, and Irina Baranova, who all came to ABT as guest artists over the years.

Between Balanchine's new brand of neoclassicism at New York City Ballet and Chase's popularizing of the classics at American Ballet Theatre, the United States in the 1960s began experiencing what ballet-watchers call a dance boom. It was kick-started in the 1950s when America and the rest of the world got its first glimpse of Russia's two giants, the touring Kirov and Bolshoi Ballets, which had been developing their ranks behind the Iron Curtain for three decades. Directly descended from the training of Petipa, Cecchetti, and Vaganova and funded generously from an early age by the Soviet state, the Russians' technical virtuosity and dramatic scope greatly impressed international audiences. Russian dancers could leap higher and spin faster than any others in the world. One in particular, Rudolf Nureyev, became known unequivocally as the greatest male dancer of his generation.

NUREYEV AND THE DANCE BOOM

After defecting to France in 1961 (complete with a dramatic standoff between the KGB and French police at a Paris airport), Nureyev soon began working with the Royal Danish Ballet in Copenhagen and the Royal Ballet in London. Though he was 19 years younger than Britain's prima ballerina Margot Fonteyn, who that same year at age 42 was nearing the normal

Rudolph Nureyev was a Russian dancer who defected to the West, and caused a sensation as a great dance talent and sex symbol. He started a dance partnership with the much older Margot Fonteyn. Despite the age difference, their chemistry made them a popular attraction.

ballet age of retirement, the Royal Ballet's artistic director Ninette de Valois saw in Fonteyn and Nureyev the makings of a legendary dance partnership. She began casting them in leading roles both in London and around the world.

Somehow it worked—the passionate, longhaired, athletic Nureyev played off the cool Fonteyn with her classic beauty and impeccable line like fire and ice. To top off the chemistry and marketing appeal of an older woman and younger man, they were actually two of the most skilled dancers in the world. Audiences flocked to see them in 1965's *Romeo and Juliet*—all the more amazing considering the 46-year-old Fonteyn was dancing the role of 14-year-old Juliet! Their tours did as much to popularize ballet in the 1960s as Anna Pavlova's had earlier in the century. Ultimately their partnership prolonged Fonteyn's career by more than a decade as she danced well into her fifties—an unsurpassed achievement for a ballerina. Nureyev himself continued to draw crowds well into the 1980s when he became artistic director of the Paris Opera Ballet.

Other Russian defectors contributed to America's dance boom as well. The two most notable figures were Natalia Makarova, a petite dancer of supreme flexibility and strength, and Mikhail Baryshnikov, a technical virtuoso who was Nureyev's rival for the title of world's best. Both Makarova and Baryshnikov joined the American Ballet Theatre upon leaving the Soviet Union. After many years of dancing and creating new works, Baryshnikov became its artistic director upon Chase's retirement in 1980.

Thus by 1980 America's ballet movement was in full swing with its own imported international stars, several large urban companies such as the San Francisco Ballet and the Boston Ballet, and its own uniquely American neo-classic vision. When New York City Ballet toured Russia in 1962, an interviewer said to Balanchine, "Welcome to Moscow, home of the classic dance."

"I beg your pardon," replied Mr. B. "Russia is the home of the romantic ballet. The home of classic ballet is now America."[3]

6

Ballet Goes Pop

THE BIRTH OF MODERN DANCE

In order to fully understand how ballet changed and became much more interesting and accessible to the general public in the late twentieth century, we first have to go back and look at modern dance and its progenitor, Isadora Duncan, at the turn of the twentieth century.

In a time when Petipa's traditional romantic style still held sway over Europe and Russia, Duncan, a freethinking American with a love of music and ancient Greek culture, brought a completely new aesthetic to the stage. Declaring herself the enemy of ballet, whose structure she labeled superficial and elitist, she instead embraced a form of dance that was its opposite: natural, free, and unbounded by rules. She toured all over Europe and Russia, dancing alone, barefoot, and dressed in long filmy tunics. The only traditional aspect of her performances was the music she

Modern dance pioneer Isadora Duncan performing a classical Greek dance. Duncan's "anti-ballet" position, embraced by other modern dance artists such as Martha Graham, led to a completely new expression of dance—an influence that would creep into ballet as well.

chose—symphonic works by great composers such as Mendelssohn, Beethoven, and Chopin. Running, hopping, and improvising wildly with great freedom in her upper body, Duncan never failed to rouse audiences—a few hated her, but most loved her, and none could deny her authentic emotional expression.

Though Duncan died in 1927 after a tumultuous and often tragic life, others further developed her ideas. The first were Ruth St. Denis and Doris Humphrey, followed by Martha Graham, the doyenne of modern dance.

Graham not only eschewed ballet's turnout and historical positioning of the feet, as Duncan had earlier, but she completely invented her own style—angular, athletic, centered in the pelvis and low back, with a low center of gravity as opposed to ballet's airborne quality. Her dances expressed primal psychological states and the female psyche in particular. In fact, men did not appear in her company at all during its first decade in the 1930s. Still, even by then, modern dance was not so much ballet's enemy as a new branch on the tree of theatrical dance. Graham and other modernists insisted their dancers take ballet class as foundation training, which is still standard practice in modern dance companies.

Not only did modern dancers thus dabble in ballet, but soon ballet choreographers began incorporating into their work such modern techniques as parallel and flexed feet and sensual, almost acrobatic moves of the body against the floor. Even Balanchine collaborated with Graham in their jointly choreographed *Episodes* in 1959.

MODERN MINGLES WITH BALLET

One of the first classical choreographers to "loosen up" ballet was American-born Jerome Robbins, who studied modern, Spanish, and Oriental dance as well as ballet in his youth. Early in his career, which included many Broadway musicals and a stint as New York City Ballet's ballet master alongside Balanchine, he created his masterpiece for American Ballet Theatre. *Fancy Free*, which premiered during the height of World War II in 1944, featured three sailors on leave dancing to the music of Leonard Bernstein. Its combination of classical ballet steps and modern, jazzy Broadway moves marked Robbins' style for decades to come and was a sign of how modern and classical lines had blurred into what has been called "crossover ballet."

Another early creator of crossover ballets was Robert Joffrey, who also studied modern dance in addition to his ballet training at the School of American Ballet. When Joffrey founded his own company in the 1960s, he focused on two things: restaging the classics of Nijinsky, Fokine and others; and commissioning modern dance choreographers to work with his company. He started the trend of ballet companies turning to modern choreographers for inspiration and variety.

One of Joffrey's commissions proved a pivotal point in the dialogue between ballet and modern dance. In 1973, dancer

FANCY FREE

Choreography by Jerome Robbins, 1944

Music by Leonard Bernstein

In addition to being highly entertaining, *Fancy Free* is historically important as the first ballet created by Robbins, the first American-born choreographer. For these reasons it has become known as a uniquely American masterwork. With only one act, which takes place on a summer night in New York City, and six characters—three sailors, two women and a bartender—*Fancy Free* became an instant hit with audiences who needed a respite from World War II. Robbins mixed classical ballet moves with popular dances of the day while Bernstein's jazzy score blared in the background. Accessible and yet highly structured, the ballet was so popular it was made into a Broadway musical called *On the Town*, also choreographed by Robbins, and later a film of the same name.

and choreographer Twyla Tharp—who had studied ballet with Antony Tudor and modern dance with Graham and others—made *Deuce Coupe* for Joffrey, set to the music of the Beach Boys. Three years later, American Ballet Theatre commissioned her work *Push Comes to Shove*, starring the inimitable Baryshnikov. Seeing the world's best male ballet dancer performing the relaxed, highly entertaining moves of Tharp gave the ballet world a populist jolt. It turned out that ballet dancers loved to work in the modern vein just as much as modern choreographers loved to fit their work onto the well-trained and highly skilled bodies of ballet dancers, and audiences approved as well.

THE BALLET SCENE TODAY

By the end of the 1970s, many a classical ballet company was incorporating modern steps into its repertoire and hiring modern choreographers to construct distinctive works on its own dancers, which the company would then pepper into its repertoire of classics during a given season. One of the most acclaimed choreographers of the 1980s was Mark Morris, a young dancer who had studied flamenco and folk styles before forming his own modern dance company. His *L'allegro, Il Penseroso et il Moderato*, though performed barefoot by dancers of varying shapes and sizes, became an instant classic because of its subject matter (two of the four medieval temperaments previously seen in Balanchine's ballet), its length (two and a half hours), and the musicality of Morris' choreography to a baroque score by Handel. In yet more evidence of the intermarriage of ballet and modern, Morris and Baryshnikov co-founded the modern White Oak Dance Project in 1990.

In addition to an influx of young choreographers who burst on the scene in the 1980s and 1990s creating modernized works for classical ballet companies, another trend developed. Troupes such as Pilobolus, Momix, Parsons Dance Company,

PUSH COMES TO SHOVE

Choreography by Twyla Tharp, 1976

Music by Joseph Lamb and Franz Joseph Haydn

If *Fancy Free* planted the seed of crossover ballet, *Push Comes to Shove* was crossover in full bloom 32 years later. Twyla Tharp, who had trained in both ballet and modern dance—the latter with Martha Graham and Graham disciple Paul Taylor—created a complete intermingling of classical ballet steps with modern dance for American Ballet Theatre. Alternating between the rococo strains of Haydn's Symphony No. 82 and the ragtime piano of Joseph Lamb, *Push* features a male lead (originally Mikhail Baryshnikov, who helped make it a success), two female leads representing the two feminine ideals of classical ballet—the tall, elegant ballerina and the shorter, livelier one—and a small group of dancers who comprise a corps. Combining traditional leaps and pirouettes with slinky, loose steps and turns, and incorporating many heightened pauses when the dancers seem to ponder the music as well as their own dancing, *Push* surprises audiences. There are unexpected props like a bowler hat and misplaced happenings such as a pair of dancers continuing on in silence after the music has ended or taking their bows in the middle of a dance. Though "abstract" and storyless, Tharp's choreography seems to ask questions about ballet itself, such as, "What if the man competes with the woman instead of lifting and supporting her?" and "Do the steps always have to sync up with the music?" Tharp's sharp, witty moves create a thoughtful but also entertaining dance that ultimately leaves the audience reeling in laughter as well as applause.

Mark Morris, a modern dance choreographer, formed a dance company called the White Oak Dance Project with Mikhail Baryshnikov, further melding the worlds of modern dance and ballet. Here, Morris performs in his own interpretation of *The Nutcracker* titled *The Hard Nut*.

and many others began to skew the focus of their dances toward acrobatics, gymnastics, visual effects, optical illusion, and comedy. Often very imaginative costuming or scenery help to bring these works to life, and the dancing is very athletic. Though they would not be classified as ballet per se, these types of works lure audiences to the world of theatrical dance with their accessibility and focus on entertainment.

In short, the balletgoer now has the widest possible array of choices. Nearly every U.S. city has its own professional ballet, and even nonmetropolitan areas have developed regional troupes. Several of the major national and international companies tour regularly. Today's balletgoers can see a traditional staging of *The Nutcracker* or Morris' *The Hard Nut*, a comic retelling of the Christmas classic. He can see the Joffrey Ballet perform its restaging of Nijinsky's infamous *L'Sacre du Printemps* or its 1992 ballet *Billboards*, set to the music of Prince. He can see the classical *Swan Lake* or opt for Matthew Bourne's version featuring a male Odette/Odile "swan queen" and a cast of all-male swans: barefoot, muscular, and faces painted with ominous black beaks.

A NEW DEFINITION

With all this crossover going on, how does one know the difference between ballet, modern dance, and other kinds of dancing such as the Irish step and folk dances featured in the popular *Riverdance*?

In strictly traditional terms, ballet must adhere to the rules of the *danse d'école* established in France in the seventeenth century. Some of those conventions include turnout, the defined vocabulary of steps such as jetés and arabesques, pointed feet, ballet line, and women dancing en pointe. These days, most choreographers take the artistic liberty of bending those rules, creating all kinds of interesting and neverending combinations of movement. As long as the choreographer and the dancers work from the rules as a foundation—even if bending them a bit—the work is often classified as ballet.

At its core, though, ballet is not merely about rules. The rules exist only to serve its real purpose: to present the human body at its height of strength, beauty and grace—qualities that dancers and choreographers train for decades to develop using the language of turnout, extension, and line.

There is something else, however, at the heart of ballet. Its emotional center is sensual and romantic—some would say even sexual. If it is a classic in the vein of Petipa that one watches, the old-fashioned notion of chivalry is no doubt playing a huge part in both the storyline and the dancing

Choreographer and dancer Jerome Robbins (third from right) created the very American ballet *Fancy Free*, a crossover ballet that employed a jazzy score by Leonard Bernstein. It was so popular that it later became a Broadway musical and film called *On The Town*.

itself: the strong man supporting and protecting the woman and the woman displaying an ethereal feminine grace. In more modern fare, there are fewer gender roles at play, but they are replaced with a raw bodily energy that is more honest and natural. From any viewpoint, ballet is about the body—the bodies of men and women either in an ideal form similar to a moving sculpture or in more natural and vulnerable form. The bodies are always beautiful and, like all art, their movements create emotion—and sometimes new ways of looking at the world.

Moving into the twenty-first century, ballet is bound to spread in even more imaginative directions. Though the great classics continue to thrive, one can assume that dance makers will bend even more rules. This does not mean however that at some point in the far future toe shoes and the five positions will be retired.

A world without dancers performing *Swan Lake* would be akin to a world without actors doing *Hamlet* or a world without musicians playing Beethoven. Though it may expand far afield of its origins, as long as music inspires and physical strength and beauty enthrall people, ballet is bound to survive—carrying forward both its Old World traditions and charms as well as its modern bursts of imagination.

A Basic
Ballet Class

So what does ballet look like? What is it actually composed of?
All the mechanics of ballet are evident in a typical class, the
structure of which is consistent throughout the world, regard-
less of country, teacher or even the particular school of ballet
being taught.

At any large ballet school, and even at most smaller
regional schools meant to train nonprofessionals, the ballet
class is accompanied by live piano. In some instances, the
teacher will use a recorded album of piano accompaniment,
but the presence of a pianist serves two important aims: it
keeps up a spontaneous, non-interrupted flow of accompaniment to the dancers' work—for often the teacher will stop
mid-exercise to illustrate or correct, or want to change the
tempo—and it trains the dancer on a daily basis to work in
sync with live classical music.

Ballet classes are typically accompanied by live piano in order to provide instant accompaniment to the dancers' movements and train the dancers to work with live music.

THE BARRE

Ballet class begins at the *barre*—a thin wooden pole running parallel to the walls of the room a little above waist level. With the support of the barre dancers work one side of the body at a time, first holding on with the left hand and working the right leg (in which case the right is called "the working leg" while the left is "the supporting leg"), then turning and holding on with the right hand to work the left leg. When considering the strain of 180-degree turnout and how long it takes to train the lower body into this mold while maintaining balance, the importance of the barre becomes evident. (Try it. Turn your feet all the way out so that the toes point away from each other in a straight line. Chances are you'll begin to lose your balance, even more so if you try to move one foot anywhere while keeping the supporting leg turned out.)

Barre exercises begin with *plié*, the bending of the knees to warm up the leg muscles. Pliés are done in first, second, third, fourth and fifth positions. A bend while keeping the heels on the floor is called demi-plié; a full deep bend allowing the heels to lift is grand plié.

Dancers then proceed to *tendu* (or *battement tendu*), in which the working leg pushes out from first position until the heel lifts off the floor into an arched point to the front, side and back. Though they look like small, simple movements, tendus develop the beginning of a dancer's point, extension and line, training the legs to move out from and back into two most important positions of the feet—first and fifth—while keeping the rest of the body tall, centered and stationary. Thus teachers spend a great deal of time on them.

Battement tendu then proceeds to *battement dégagé*, which looks similar except the leg is brushed slightly off the floor; and to *grand battement*, in which the leg extends far up into the air.

Barre work also includes *retiré*, in which the working leg is bent and lifted so that the pointed toe touches the inner knee of the supporting leg (later this position will be used for pirouettes); and *port de bras*, or "carriage of the arms," in which the working arm moves through its own five positions;

as well as *grand port de bras* during which the dancer bends the upper body all the way forward to the floor and then all the way up into a deep backbend while working the arms. The positioning of the arms, the exact curve of the elbow and wrist, and especially the placement of each finger are matters of debate among the different ballet schools and their various teachers.

This is another instance of the great importance placed on the visual line in which the arms and hands play such a vital role. In general, the arms are softly curved from a relaxed shoulder and rounded elbow with the wrist higher than the fingers. The fingers gently curve and extend so that the very tip of the dancer's line does not end abruptly but seems to trace off into the air around her. The thumb is generally held a few inches from the other fingers, the middle finger curves in the most, and the pinky and index fingers curve the least.

It may seem picky, but even a first-time balletgoer would be sure to notice a dancer whose arms and hands were held stiffly or straight instead of curving in this way. Indeed, the goal of port de bras is to convey an always graceful, relaxed and flowing carriage of the arms, no matter how difficult the step that the lower body is attempting. A dancer may be performing a giant leap, several pirouettes, or trying with all her might to balance for several seconds on the tiptoes of one foot, but her upper body must never betray her effort. It must look relaxed, tall, and confident as the athleticism unfolds below. This holds true for the neck, head, eyes, and face as well, which are often slightly angled away from the direction of the lower body's movement in order to offset the visual line, adding a touch of panache to the step.

At some point in barre work the dancer will begin to lift either the supporting foot or both feet into *relevé*, in which the heel lifts high off the floor and the foot arches. In the case

Dancers at the barre in class showing the *relevé* position, in which the heel lifts high off the ground and the foot arches.

of men and women who are not yet working en pointe, the body balances high on the ball of the foot. In the case of women dancers taking classes in their pointe shoes, relevé proceeds all the way up to pointe so that the entire foot is arched. If the curve of the arm and hand illustrate the top of the dancer's line, the foot in relevé is the basis for the bottom of it—and a perfectly arched foot balanced inside a long satin toe shoe produces quite a stunning visual effect.

ADAGIO

As the dancers leave the support of the barre and move into center or "floorwork," the difficulty increases. Their sole support and balance must now come from a strong center, which emanates from straight legs in a tight fifth position; a pulled-in stomach and tucked-under pelvis so that there is no arch in the back (forming as straight a line as possible); and a lifted chest and head. Even when standing still, a dancer should feel that an invisible cord is running up through her body and out of her head, pulling her toward the ceiling.

Floorwork begins with *adagio*—slow, graceful steps that focus on balance, line, extension and control. In *développés*, the pointed toe of the working leg traces its way up the supporting leg, extends high to either the front, side, or back and then is held in the extended position—much like a kick in very slow motion. More than any other step, développés show a dancer's extension, or how high she can lift and hold an extended leg away from her body while keeping proper form (hips and shoulders squared). Though audiences may not know the technical name, good extension is quite easy to appreciate even for a first-time balletgoer. High extensions in second position—straight out to the side—are especially difficult and impressive. Most people have seen a photo of a ballerina with a straight leg extended up toward her ear.

Adagio inevitably includes arabesques and their counter-part, attitudes. In arabesque, the leg is lifted straight behind the torso, with the arms usually moving through various positions. A dancer's line can perhaps best be seen in her arabesque. Both the supporting leg—whether flat on the floor or en pointe—and the working leg are turned out, the working hip is lifted only enough to allow the leg to reach higher, the shoulders are square, arms curved and soft, and chin lifted. Finally, the lifted foot is completely pointed, preferably with the toe angled higher than the heel. All these details can seem mundane, but remember that ballet's goal is to trace beautiful angles, curves, and patterns with the body. The difference between an arabesque that does not employ them and one that does is quite obvious to the eye; the former will look clumsy and stilted, the latter symmetrical and uplifted.

Attitude (the position invented by Carlo Blasis) is much like arabesque except that the lifted leg is bent at the knee instead of straight. Unlike arabesque, attitude can also be performed in front of the body or to the side, not only in back.

ALLEGRO

The adagio portion of the class gives way to *allegro*, a faster, livelier set of steps that focus on turning and leap-ing. Jetés, which translate simply as "thrown," are the groundwork for much of allegro. They are leaps from one foot to the other and can be done in any direction. They can be small and almost unnoticeable onstage or take the form of *grand jeté*, the huge running leap dancers take which frequently features a mid-air split. *Grand jeté en tournant* is a large jeté performed while the dancer spins her body in the air.

Pirouettes, turns on one leg with the other lifted usually toe to knee (though the lifted leg can also be extended in attitude

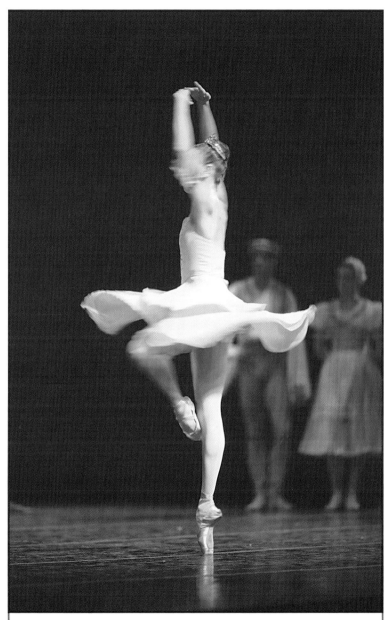

One of the best-known ballet moves is the *pirouette*, in which turns are made on one leg while the other leg is bent so that its toe is near the supporting leg's knee.

or often second position), are practiced during adagio too. Pirouettes are an art and science all to themselves and take many years to master. Multiple pirouettes are even more difficult, and definitely one of the steps an audience looks for in a performance. The most virtuosic form of pirouettes are *fouettés*, in which the working leg does not touch the ground between turns but whips out to the side before pulling in for the next rotation. Both *Swan Lake* and *Don Quixote* feature scenes in which the lead ballerina performs 32 fouettés uninterrupted, usually finishing off the last one with a multiple pirouette for flourish to loud applause.

Unlike pirouettes, which originate from the standing leg simply by lifting the working leg, *piqué turns* involve the dancer throwing a leg out and then turning onto it. When a ballerina completes a solo performing fast turns with one leg bent to the knee while moving in a large circular pattern around the stage, she is doing piqués. *Piqué* is a step in and of itself and consists simply of moving in any direction from plié onto one straight leg in relevé; it is the main way dancers move themselves about the stage.

Piqué turns often give way to *chainés*, a series of very fast turns in which the legs are kept close together and the weight moves quickly and almost imperceptibly from foot to foot. When a dancer finishes off a solo with spins that look like she is twirling on ice or unwinding like a spool of thread, she is performing chainés.

Entrechats are another virtuosic step, performed mainly by male dancers. They begin in fifth position plié from which the dancer jumps straight into the air, beating his feet in a quick "exchange" front to back, as many times as possible, before landing. In *entrechat dix*, the maximum achieved so far, the legs cross six times in the air.

Tours, another specialty of the men, involve leaving the floor from plié into a high, straight spin of the body, ending in plié. Both tours and entrechats show a dancer's strength and elevation, or what is often called his "attack," and multiple tours can be quite breathtaking to witness onstage.

Ballet class ends with *reverence*—traditional bows (for the men) or low curtsies (for the women) to the teacher. This is not a quick thank-you but a long, slow bending to the ballet master, steeped in decorum and performed to music, which also gives the dancers practice for graceful bowing onstage.

Glossary

Adagio (uh-dah-zheo) Slow and sustained movements performed during the second part of a ballet class and focused on balance and control; a slow and sustained dance in a ballet.

Allegro (uh-leh-gro) Fast running and jumping movements performed during the last part of a ballet class; a fast, lively dance in a ballet.

Arabesque (ara-besk) A common position in which the weight of the body is supported on one leg while the other is extended in back, knee straight. The arabesque may be varied in many ways by changing the position of the arms, the angle of the body and the height of the leg in the air.

Attitude A classical position similar to the arabesque, except the knee of the raised leg is bent.

Balancé (ba-lohn-say) A waltz step. On a count of 1-2-3, the working leg steps to the side in plié (1), the supporting leg follows behind, stepping onto the ball of the foot (2), and then the weight is transferred to the working leg again (3). Balancés can also be done to the front and back or turning.

Ballet master An old-fashioned term synonymous with *choreographer.*

Ballon (ba-lahn) The appearance of weightlessness and of being airborne. A dancer is said to have ballon if he seems to be in the air constantly with only momentary contact with the floor.

Barre (bar) A long wooden pole attached to the walls of a dance studio upon which dancers traditionally do warm-up exercises.

Battement (baht-mahn) An extension of the leg. Some variations are *grand battement* and *petit battement.*

Battement tendu (tahn-du) An exercise in which the working foot slides out from either first or fifth position to a pointed toe, never leaving the floor. Critical for learning to move the foot quickly and gracefully while maintaining placement, Balanchine considered it the most important exercise in all of ballet. Also simply called *tendu.*

Bourée (boo-ray) A rapid traveling step, like a trill on the points of the toes, with the feet in fifth position. The feet move so quickly that the transfer of weight is almost imperceptible and the ballerina seems to skim across the stage.

Center exercises Exercises done freely in the center of the room, as opposed to those done with the support of the barre.

Chainé (sheh-nay) A series of turns, executed in a line or in a circle, in which the feet remain together and the weight is transferred rapidly and almost imperceptibly from one foot to the other as the body revolves.

Changement (shahnj-mahn) A jump, straight up, starting from fifth position with one foot in front and landing in fifth position with the other foot in front.

Chassé (shah-say) A slide in which the weight is transferred from two feet to one, or from one to another.

Choreographer The person who creates, or composes, dance.

Coda The final section of a pas de deux in which the partners reunite to fast, lively music.

Corps de ballet (cor-du-ba-ley) The supporting dancers of the ballet company whose role is often to perform group dances in unison.

Croisé (kwah-seh) A position on stage in which the dancer faces one of the front corners with the legs crossed.

Danseur (dan-sir) A professional male dancer.

Derrière (dare-ay-air) Directed behind the body.

Devant (day-vahn) Directed in front of the body.

Développé (deh-vel-oh-pay) A smooth, gradual unfolding of the leg toward the front, side or back. The working leg is drawn up to the knee of the supporting leg and from there smoothly out to a position in the air, usually at 90 degrees or higher.

Divertissement (dee-vert-tis-mahn) Meaning "diversion," a typically short dance in a classical ballet that has little to do with the plot but provides variety for the audience. Examples of divertissements are the themed dances in Act II of *The Nutcracker* and Act III of *Swan Lake.*

Elevation The ability to jump high in the air. A step of elevation is a jump.

En dedans (on day-dahn) Used to describe motion toward the front of the body. In a pirouette en dedans, for example, the dancer turns so the raised leg rotates toward the front.

En dehors (on day-or) Used to describe motion away from the front of the body. In a pirouette en dehors, for example, the dancer turns so the raised leg rotates away from the front.

En face (on fah-say) A position on stage facing directly forward, toward the audience.

En l'air (on lair) Used to describe movements in which the working leg is raised a considerable distance off the ground.

En pointe (on point) On the tips of the toes. Originally dancers did this in soft slippers; today toe shoes are blocked across the toe section to give added support.

Entrechat (ahn-treh-shah) A jump beginning and ending in fifth position. While the body is in the air, the feet are rapidly crossed two or more times.

Épaulement (eh-pahl-mahn) Rotation of the shoulders and head, relative to the hips, to add beauty or expressiveness to a pose, step, or movement.

Extension The ability to raise the working leg high in the air. Good extension comes from a combination of inborn flexibility and training.

Fondu (fahn-du) Any movement that lowers the body by bending only the supporting leg, as opposed to a plié in which both legs bend.

Fouetté (fweh-tay) One of the most brilliant steps in ballet. The dancer repeatedly turns on one foot (usually en pointe) as in pirouette, but between each revolution the working leg whips sharply into second position *en l'air* (in the air.)

French School The school of classical ballet known for its elegance and grace as opposed to technical strength and virtuosity.

Glissade (glih-sahd) A sliding step, beginning and ending in fifth position, usually done to the side.

Grand battement (grahn-baht-mahn) A "kick" in which the working leg is raised as high as possible while keeping the rest of the body still. The movement is controlled as the leg lifts and as it comes down; the leg cannot be thrown.

Grand jeté (grahn-zheh-tay) A long horizontal jump, usually forward, starting from one leg and landing on the other. In the middle of the jump, the dancer may be doing a split in midair. One of the most memorable of all ballet jumps; the dancer seems to float in the air.

Grand pas de deux See *pas de deux.*

Italian School The school of ballet known for its high jumps, multiple turns and athletic strength. Its master teacher was Enrico Cecchetti.

Jeté (zheh-tay) A jump from one foot to the other foot, throwing the working leg out and then landing on it. The most common variation is a *grand jeté.*

Labanotation A system of dance notation that attempts to diagram choreography in a way similar to music notation in order to document it for the future. Developed in the 1920s by Rudolf Laban, it is one of few notational systems for dance, none of which are widely used or understood. Most choreography is passed down orally, today with the help of film and video.

Line The harmonious alignment of the various parts of the dancer's body, the visual trace of which extends outward from the limbs in every direction, beyond them.

Pas de chat (pah-deh-shah) Literally translates as "leap of the cat," a pas de chat is a fast jump in which first one leg, then the other quickly leave the ground with the knees bent, giving the effect of the legs forming a diamond shape in mid-air. In the famous "Dance of the Cygnets" in *Swan Lake* the four cygnets perform 16 pas de chat.

Pas de deux (pah deh duh) Literally "step for two," a duet, often in several sections, beginning with a partnered adagio, followed by the man's allegro, the woman's allegro and finally the coda. Sometimes called a *grand pas de deux.*

Penché (pahn-shay) A tilting of the body to achieve an extreme pose. An example is when the dancer is in an arabesque at 90 degrees, then pushes her working leg upward and the body down to achieve a much greater angle between legs, often resulting in a 180-degree split.

Piqué (pee-kay) A step up onto one foot with the other foot lifted to the knee or in the air.

Pirouette (pir-roh-wet) A turn in place, on one foot. A good dancer can execute four or five continuous revolutions; a virtuoso, as many as a dozen. During multiple pirouettes, the dancer uses spotting to avoid becoming disoriented. Pirouettes are usually fast, but supported pirouettes, in which a partner steadies the soloist at the waist or by a hand above the head, may be done very slowly.

Plié (plee-ay) A bend of the knees, normally the first exercise done in ballet class. *Demi-plié* is a small bend with the heels on the floor; *grand plié* is a deep bend to where the thighs are nearly horizontal.

Pointe See *en pointe.*

Pointe shoes See *toe shoes.*

Port de bras (por-deh-brah) The carriage of the arms. In grand port de bras, the dancer also moves the torso along with the arms, bending all the way down to the floor, then back up and then backward in a slight backbend.

Relevé (re-leh-vay) A movement in which the heels are raised off the floor. The rise may be smooth or aided by a slight spring. If wearing soft shoes, the dancer balances on the ball of the foot. If wearing pointe shoes, she balances on the tip of the toes.

Retiré (reh-teer-ay) A position in which the working foot is drawn up to the knee of the supporting leg.

Rond de jambe (rohn deh jahm) A circular movement of the leg, accomplished either with the toe on the floor or with the working leg raised.

Russian School The school of classical ballet that combined elements of French gracefulness and Italian athleticism. Its methods of instruction were perfected and documented by Agrippina Vaganova with the Vaganova system.

Spotting A technique for keeping oriented and avoiding dizziness during turns. The dancer picks a spot and keeps her eyes focused on it even as the body begins to turn. When the head finally follows the body into the turn, she quickly whips it around to find the spot again.

Technique The detailed craft of dancing, built through repetition of exercises. A dancer with good technique displays proper skill in turnout, elevation, extension, line, upper body carriage, strength and endurance.

Tendu (tahn-du) Short for *battement tendu*.

Terre-à-terre (tair-ah-tair) Used to describe steps in which the dancer's feet do not leave the floor, or barely leave the floor.

Toe shoes Soft fabric (usually satin) slippers blocked across the toes with extra material and hard glue to give support when the dancer rises en pointe.

Tour en l'air (tour ahn le-air) A complete single, double or triple turn in the air, usually beginning from and ending in fifth position. It is almost always executed by male dancers.

Turnout The balletic stance in which the legs are rotated outward so that the legs (and feet) point in opposite directions, ideally in a straight line. Turnout must begin at the hip. Forcing the feet and letting the knees, legs, and hips follow puts severe strain on the joints.

Tutu The traditional ballet skirt, usually made of many layers of gathered tulle. The length of the tutu varies according to the period or style of the ballet being performed.

Vaganova system A detailed system of instruction developed by Agrippina Vaganova to develop dancers of the Russian School.

Virtuoso Though in general meaning simply having great skill, in classical ballet a virtuoso usually refers to a dancer with supreme athletic skill in particular—able to turn fast, leap high and balance for long periods—as opposed to skills of grace or presentation (though virtuosos may also possess those).

1489   A fete in Tortona, Italy includes music, recitation and self-contained dances called *entrées*.

1494   France's Charles II invades Naples and discovers Italian court dances called *balli*.

1533   Catherine D'Medici marries Henry II of France, merging French court life with Italian *balli*.

1581   *Le Ballet Comique de la Reine*, the first court ballet, is staged by D'Medici's for a relative's wedding.

1584   Teatro d'Olympico in Verona, Italy opens with a proscenium arch stage.

1605   Masques (English court ballets) begin to appear in London.

1651   King Louis XIV appears as Apollo in *Le Ballet de la Nuit*.

1661   Louis XIV creates the Academie Royale de Danse.

1669   Louis XIV creates Academie Royale de la Musique (Paris Opera) run by Jean-Baptiste Lully. Ballet moves from the palace ballroom to a proscenium arch theater.

1681   The first professional female dancer, Madamoiselle Lafontaine, appears in *Le Triomphe de l'Amour* in Paris.

1726   Marie Camargo makes her debut in Paris.

1727   Marie Sallé makes her debut in Paris.

1738   Empress Anna Ivanovna founds Imperial Ballet School in St. Petersburg, Russia, directed by Jean-Baptise Landé.

1758   Jean Georges-Noverre begins producing *ballets d'action*.

1760   Noverre publishes his *Letters on the Dance*.

1781   Noverre is appointed ballet master at King's Theatre in London.

1789   Jean Dauberval's *La Fille Mal Gardée* premieres in Bordeaux, France.

1789   The French Revolution takes place.

1796   Charles-Louis Didelot produces *Flora and Zephyr* in London, which introduced dancing from wires, or "flying ballet."

1813   Imperale Regio Academia di Danze established at La Scala in Milan, Italy.

1820   Carlo Blasis writes *An Elementary Treatise upon the Theory and Practice of the Art of Dancing.*

1825   Moscow's Bolshoi Theater opens.

1830   Blasis publishes *The Code of Terpsichore.*

1832   Marie Taglioni dances *en pointe* in *La Sylphide* in Paris.

1834   Fanny Elssler debuts at Paris Opera.

1837   Blasis appointed director of La Scala's dance academy.

1841   *Giselle* by Jean Coralli and Jules Perrot premieres in Paris starring Carlotta Grisi.

1869   Marius Petipa's *Don Quixote* premieres in Moscow.

1870   Petipa named ballet master at Imperial Ballet in St. Petersburg.

1877   Petipa's *La Bayadere* premieres in St. Petersburg.

1890   Petipa's *The Sleeping Beauty* premieres in St. Petersburg; Enrico Cecchetti becomes dancer and ballet master at Russia's Imperial Ballet, along with Petipa.

1892   Petipa's *The Nutcracker* premieres in St. Petersburg.

1895   Petipa and Lev Ivanov premiere *Swan Lake* in St. Petersburg.

1905 Pavlova performs Michael Fokine's *The Dying Swan* in St. Petersburg.

1909 Serge Diaghilev present Ballets Russes' first season in Paris.

1910 Chicago Opera Ballet established.

1912 Vaslav Nijinsky debuts *L'apres-midi d'un Faune* for Ballets Russes.

1917 The Russian Revolution takes place; Agrippina Vaganova begins teaching at the Kirov Ballet.

1924 George Balanchine joins Ballet Russes.

1931 Ninette de Valois becomes director of the Vic-Wells Ballet (later renamed Sadler's Wells Ballet in 1935 and Royal Ballet in 1956).

1933 San Francisco Ballet founded by Adolph Bolm.

1934 Balanchine and Lincoln Kirstein found School of American Ballet; Margot Fonteyn debuts with the Vic-Wells Ballet in London; Vaganova publishes *Fundamentals of the Classic Dance* in Russia.

1935 Balanchine premieres *Serenade* in New York.

1940 Lucia Chase and Richard Pleasant found American Ballet Theatre in New York.

1944 Jerome Robbins premieres *Fancy Free* in New York.

1948 Birth of New York City Ballet.

1956 Bolshoi Ballet's first appearance in New York; Joffrey Ballet established.

1957 Balanchine's *Agon* premieres in New York.

1961 Kirov Ballet begins touring the West.

1962 Rudoff Nureyev joins Royal Ballet and begins partner-
      ship with Fonteyn.

1964 Virginia Williams founds Boston Ballet.

1965 Balanchine's *Don Quixote* premieres in New York;
      Fonteyn and Nureyev appear in Frederick Ashton's
      Romeo and Juliet in London.

1967 Balanchine's *Jewels* premieres in New York.

1971 Dance Theatre of Harlem gives its first performance.

1974 Mikhail Baryshnikov defects to the West.

1976 Twyla Tharp choreographs *Push Comes to Shove*,
      considered one of the first crossover ballets, for the
      American Ballet Theatre.

1980 Baryshnikov becomes artistic director of the American
      Ballet Theatre.

1983 Balanchine dies, leaving Peter Martins as ballet master-
      in-chief of the New York City Ballet; Nureyev becomes
      artistic director of the Paris Opera Ballet.

1993 Nureyev dies.

The following videos are available at either *www.amazon.com* or through Kultur Video at *www.kulturvideo.com* or 800-573-3782.

American Ballet Theatre Now: Variety and Virtuosity and *American Ballet Theatre Now: Highlights from the ABT Repertoire*, prod. and dir. by Judy Kinberg, 83 minutes, WNET/Dance In America, 1998, videocassette.

The Balanchine Celebration, Parts I and II, prod. by Judy Kinberg, dir. by Matthew Diamond, 172 minutes, WNET/Dance In America, 1996, videocassette. Starring Darcy Bussell, Patricia Barker and others.

Balanchine's *The Nutcracker*, prod. by Robert A. Krasnow and Robert Hurwitz, dir. by Emile Ardolino, 93 minutes, Warner Home Video, 1993, videocassette. Starring Darci Kistler, Damian Woetzel and Macaulay Culkin.

Ballet Favorites, 90 minutes, Kultur Video, 1999, videocassette. Starring Mikhail Baryshnikov, Darcy Bussell and others.

Billy Elliot, prod. by Jon Finn and Greg Brenman, dir. by Stephen Daldry, 110 minutes, Universal Studios, 2000, videocassette. Starring Jamie Bell.

Fonteyn and Nureyev: The Perfect Partnership, prod. and dir. by Peter Batty, 90 minutes, Kultur Video, 1988, videocassette. Starring Margot Fonteyn and Rudolf Nureyev.

Giselle with Ballet Teatro al La Scala, 116 minutes, Image Entertainment, 1996, videocassette. Starring Alessandra Ferri and Massimo Murru.

The Glory of the Bolshoi, prod. by Julia Matheson and Carl Simons, 96 minutes, Kultur Video, 1995, videocassette. Starring dancers of the Bolshoi Ballet.

The Glory of the Kirov, prod. by Julia Matheson and Carl Simons, 91 minutes, Kultur Video, 1995, videocassette. Starring dancers of the Kirov Ballet.

The New York City Ballet Workout, prod. and dir. by Richard Blanshard, 90 minutes, Palm Pictures, 2000, videocassette.

Swan Lake with the Kirov Ballet, dir. by Colin Nears, 116 minutes, Kultur Video, 1996, videocassette. Starring Yulia Makhalina and Igor Zelensky.

Natalia Makarova's Tchaikovsky: Swan Lake with the London Festival Ballet, prod. and dir. by Thomas Grimm, 116 minutes, Kultur Video, 1997, videocassette.

The Video Dictionary of Classical Ballet, prod. and dir. by Robert Beck, 270 minutes, Kultur Video,1985, videocassette. Featuring Merrill Ashley, Denis Jackson, Kevin McKenzie and Georgina Parkinson.

American Ballet Theatre
www.abt.org

Andros on Ballet
androsdance.tripod.com/home.html

Ballet Alert
www.balletalert.com

The Electric Ballerina
www.novia.net/~jlw/electric/electric.html

England's Royal Ballet
www.ballet.co.uk

The History of Ballet
www.ccs.neu.edu/home/yiannis/dance/history.html

New York City Ballet
www.nycb.com

San Francisco Ballet
www.sfb.org

The-Ballet.com
www.the-ballet.com

Bibliography

Acocella, Joan (editor). *The Diary of Vaslav Nijinsky*. New York: Farrar, Straus and Giroux, 1999.

Boorstin, Daniel. *The Creators: A History of the Heroes of the Imagination*. New York, Vintage Books, 1992.

Clarke, Mark and Clement Crisp. *Ballet: An Illustrated History*. New York: Universe Books, 1973.

Craine, Debra and Judith Mackrell. *The Oxford Dictionary of Dance*. New York: Oxford University Press, 2000.

Greskovic, Robert. *Ballet 101: A Complete Guide to Learning and Loving the Ballet*. New York: Hyperion, 1998.

Gruen, John. *The Private World of Ballet*. New York: Viking Press, 1975.

Ryman, Rhonda. *Dictionary of Classical Ballet Terminology*. Hightstown, NJ: Princeton Book Company, 1997.

Schorer, Suki. *Suki Schorer on Balanchine Technique*. New York: Knopf, 1999.

Steeh, Judith. *History of Ballet and Modern Dance*. New York: Galahad Books, 1982.

Taper, Bernard. *Balanchine: A Biography*. Berkeley: University of California Press, 1984.

Acocella, Joan (editor). *Baryshnikov in Black and White* (pictorial). New York: Bloomsbury USA, 2002.

Barber, David W. *Tutus, Tights and Tiptoes: Ballet History as It Ought to Be Taught.* Toronto, Canada: Sound & Vision Limited, 2000.

Dance Magazine, 111 Myrtle St., Suite 203, Oakland, CA 94607, 510-839-6060 or www.dancemagazine.com.

Farrell, Suzanne. *Holding on to the Air: An Autobiography.* New York: Summit Books, 1990.

Hammond, Sandra Noll. *Ballet Basics* (fourth edition). New York: McGraw-Hill, 1999.

Kent, Allegra. *Once a Dancer.* New York: St. Martin's Press, 1997.

Kirkland, Gelsey. *Dancing on My Grave: An Autobiography.* New York: Berkeley Publishing Group (division of Penguin Putnam), 1996.

Ramsey, Christopher (editor). *Tributes: Celebrating Fifty Years of the New York City Ballet* (pictorial). New York: William Morrow, 1998.

Thalia, Mara. *The Language of Ballet: A Dictionary.* Hightstown, NJ: Princeton Book Company Publishers, 1988.

Notes

Chapter 1 The Human Body as Art

1 Robert Greskovic. *Ballet 101: A Complete Guide to Learning and Loving the Ballet.* (New York: Hyperion, 1998),

Chapter 5 The Balanchine Era

1 John Gruen. *The Private World of Ballet.* (New York: Viking Press, 1975), 284.

2 Robert Greskovic. *Ballet 101: A Complete Guide to Learning and Loving the Ballet.* (New York: Hyperion, 1998), 200.

3 Gruen, loc. cit.

France, history of ballet in, 15, 28, 30-35, 38-39, 40, 42, 45, 48, 49, 50, 60, 61, 71, 79
French School, 45, 48, 50, 60
Fundamentals of Classical Dance (Vaganova), 60
Future of Ballet, 81

Germany, history of ballet in, 32
Geva, Tamara, 65
Giselle, 39-40, 42, 69
Graham, Martha, 74, 76
Grand battement, 84
Grand jeté, 22, 88
Grand jeté en tournant, 88
Grand pas de deux, 44
Grand plié, 84
Grand port de bras, 85
Greece, theatrical dancing in, 24
Gymnastics, 78

Handel, George Frederick, 76
Hands, 84-85, 87
Hard Nut, The, 79
History of ballet
    and ancient roots, 24-25
    and commoners, 35
    and court ballets, 26-28, 35
    and democracy, 35
    in England, 32, 35, 48, 49, 58-59, 69-71
    and founding fathers, 28, 30-33
    in France, 15, 28, 30-35, 38-39, 40, 42, 45, 48, 49, 50, 60, 61, 71, 79
    in Italy, 26-28, 32, 35, 36-38, 42, 45, 48, 60
    and romantic period, 36-49
    and schools of ballet, 45, 48-49, 50, 60

in Soviet Union, 59-61, 69, 71
    and women, 33-35, 36-42
    See also Russia, history of ballet in; United States, history of ballet in
Humphrey, Doris, 74

Imperial Dancing Academy, 45
Imperial Russian Ballet, 35, 42
Imperial St. Petersburg School, 35
    See also Kirov Ballet
Italian School, 45, 48, 60
Italy, history of ballet in, 26-28, 32, 35, 36-38, 42, 45, 48, 60
Ivanovna, Anna, Empress of Russia, 35

Jeté, 15, 79, 88
    grand, 22, 88
Joffrey, Robert, 75-76
Joffrey Ballet, 57, 79

Kent, Allegra, 66
Kirov Ballet, 35, 69
    See also Imperial Russian Ballet
Kirstein, Lincoln, 61, 62

Lafontaine, Mademoiselle, 33-34
LeClerq, Tanaquil, 66
Lepri, Giovanni, 45
Lettres sur la Danse et sur les Ballets (Letters on Dancing) (Noverre), 32-33
Line, 79, 84-85, 88
Louis XIV, King of France, 30-31, 45
Lully, Jean-Baptiste, 31, 33

McBride, Patricia, 66
Makarova, Natalia, 71

Index

Index

Picture Credits

About the Author

Robin Rinaldi studied ballet as a child and young adult. A former technical writer, she has written more than 30 reference books, three of which won awards from the Northern California Society of Technical Writers. As a journalist, she has written dance reviews for the *Sacramento News & Review* and *Philadelphia Weekly*, interviewing such choreographers as Mark Morris, Ron Cunningham, David Parsons, and Judith Jamison. She lives in Philadelphia, where she currently writes freelance magazine articles and a restaurant review column for *Philadelphia Weekly*.